HOW TO DISAPPEAR COMPLETELY
AND
NEVER BE FOUND

HOW TO DISAPPEAR COMPLETELY
AND
NEVER BE FOUND

by Doug Richmond

Loompanics Unlimited
Port Townsend, WA 98368

**HOW TO DISAPPEAR COMPLETELY
AND NEVER BE FOUND**
©1986 by Doug Richmond

Published by:
Loompanics Unlimited
PO Box 1197
Port Townsend, WA 98368

ISBN 0-915179-52-0
**Library of Congress
   Catalog Card Number 86-082641**

TABLE OF CONTENTS

INTRODUCTION

*"For life is not the thing we thought and not the thing we plan." —**The Harpy,** by Robert Service.*

To a man of a certain age there's a bit of magic in the very thought of cutting all ties, of getting away from it all, of changing names and jobs and women and living happily ever after in a more salubrious clime! To most it will always remain a tantalizing daydream, but for thousands upon thousands there eventually comes a day when wishes are translated into action.

The stumbling-block that holds most dreamers-of-better-things back from concrete action — in addition to a simple lack of gumption — is their lack of specific knowledge about how to establish, document, and feed a new identity.

The actual mechanics of identity change are not well known. Everyone knows how to get married or get divorced, but how many people know exactly how to establish credit in a strange town where one has only "existed" for a couple of weeks? And yet, disappearing is a relatively common phenomenon.

Perhaps it is because I, too, am a man of a certain age that I became so enchanted by a disappearance story told to me by a perfect stranger who introduced himself as "Capa," a fellow passenger on a bus from Nogales to

1

Mazatlan one spring day a few years back. When I met Capa again a half-year later in Sausalito, California, my interest in those who disappear and change identities was so stirred that I began to research this book.

I had very little success at first. The books I found in libraries were virtually worthless. To my surprise, the people in the Missing Persons section of the local police department knew so little about the subject that *they* were quizzing *me* about the techniques involved! I was so engrossed in the subject that I began talking to friends, relatives, even strangers on trains, planes, buses, in hotels and saloons, about disappearing and identity-switching. And that is where I hit paydirt!

The popular image of the disappearee is one of a sad and lonely individual who drifts from town to town full of remorse over the family and lifestyle he abandoned. In fact, the disappearees I met were quietly proud of having accomplished a very difficult gambit alone and unaided. Perhaps this is why they were willing to talk anonymously to a stranger who is obviously in sympathy with their great undertakings.

I soon found that disappearees are much more prevalent than I'd imagined and that they come from all walks of life, from multi-millionaires to laborers, from judges to grocery clerks, from ministers to army non-coms. I found that the father of one of my best friends had pulled a classic disappearance, stepping out casually one evening after supper for a pack of cigarettes, and has not been heard from since. Complete strangers in bars and over the phone recounted in extreme detail and with great pleasure how a friend (almost always a "friend") changed his identity, the stumbling blocks vaulted, the legal obstacles hurdled, the loneliness conquered.

I hit on the idea of handing out printed cards all over the San Francisco Bay area inviting people with first-hand knowledge of identity changing to call me. I received a considerable number of calls. Unfortunately, instead of people with first-hand knowledge of disappearances, I received a huge number of calls from people contemplating pulling the stunt and about an equal number from out-and-out screwballs. But I received more than enough contacts from bonafide disappearees and their immediate families to make it all worthwhile.

The calls from dreamers-about-disappearing were not a total loss. From them I received a considerable amount of background information about the situations and problems that make people seriously consider chucking it all and beginning over again.

Seven years have passed since my chance meeting with Capa. During that time I have talked with hundreds of people about the art of disappearing and switching identities. What follows is a collection of anecdotes from the lives of the disappeared showing what motivated them to leave, how they created their new identities and the way they live the new lives they have built.

While talking with the disappearees I never attempted to disguise that I was researching a book. Still, they were extremely gun-shy about notebooks and tape recorders. Therefore, the conversations recounted herein are essentially reconstructions from memory rather than verbatim quotes. In every instance there are slight changes in the stories to shield those who generously shared their thoughts and experiences.

If one of the disappearees I quote recognizes himself I'd rather like to hear from him...

WHO DISAPPEARS — AND WHY

"The Problems of Victory are more agreeable than the Problems of Defeat, but no less difficult." **—Winston Churchill**

WHO DISAPPEARS

There are no reliable statistics on the number of people who disappear each year. This is obviously due to the nature of the action, the goal of which is to remain undetected, and also to the method used to collect such statistics.

All disappearance statistics are ultimately based on "official" records of "missing persons." These records are completely unreliable because of the way they are compiled. The two main sources of error are: (1) the large number of disappearees who are never officially reported as missing persons; and (2) the smaller number of people listed as missing who are not. Let's start with the first category and see why some people are never cataloged as "missing."

A person who disappears has to be formally reported missing before the police will take any official notice. Most disappearances are reported to the Missing Persons Bureau (MPB) of the local police department. There are many reasons for truly "missing" people to go unreported.

Fugitives from the law are almost never reported as missing persons. Think about it for a minute: if you were a close relative or friend of someone who skipped bail, would you run to the nearest police station to report your relative or friend missing? Aiding a fugitive is against the law but keeping silent about his departure is not. Most people in this situation would just let the police find out in their own sweet time.

Statistics on the number of fugitives are not collected by MPB's. Federal and state law enforcement agencies usually handle such cases and it is doubtful they will ever reveal the actual number of fugitives; the reaction of Congress and the public to the huge number of criminals roaming free in this country would focus unwanted attention on their operations.

Other disappearees go unreported because nobody cares enough about them to try and find them. Many disappearees do not have broad social ties. They are loners who do not suffer from guilt or regret at leaving loved ones behind. Indeed, it is the emotional attachments people have to family, friends and co-workers that keeps those who have good reason to leave from doing so. If they do leave, it is these attachments that either force them to come back or lead to their capture.

A good example of this kind of unreported disappearee is the clever embezzler whose carefully-planned theft goes undetected. In these days of computerized finances such misappropriation of funds is easier to hide, and many companies are reluctant to admit publicly that they are vulnerable to such a crime. They may call in detectives but almost never the police.

Most adult missing persons reports are filed by wives whose husbands have ducked out. As we shall see later in this chapter, the majority of legitimate disappearances come as the final act in an unhappy marriage. There are many sensible reasons why a great number of such disappearances would go unreported.

If the relationship between husband and wife is one of mutual hatred the wife may be relieved to have "hubby" out of her life. She won't report her husband missing because she couldn't care less. In fact, she might be afraid that if she does report him missing the police will find him and bring him back — and that's the last thing on earth she desires!

A wife might feel shame that her husband left her or guilt that it was her failure as a woman that drove him away. Reporting her husband missing would force her to confront the reality of their messed-up lives. She'd rather believe he just went somewhere to cool off. Or maybe she feels if that's what he wants, fine; she'd rather work things out, but she won't interfere with his decision to leave.

For other women there is complete disbelief that their husbands would want to desert them. They are loath to report their husbands missing because of the adverse publicity: "What will the neighbors think?" Again, it is easier for them to believe that he's out on a drunk — no need to report that. As days turn to weeks turn to months she comes to accept the disappearance although she never reports it.

Those are the main reasons disappearees do not get officially reported as missing persons. Now let's look at the reasons for reporting people missing who are not. We'll start with the married couple and look at them from the other side.

It is not uncommon for a fierce argument between cohabitants to end with one of the partners slamming the front door on their way out. The police have learned through years of experience that the husband off on a hundred-dollar drunk will be back before the week is out. The wife who was so eager to run to the MPB and report him missing forgets to notify them of his return amidst all the apologies. In some cases the police stumble on someone who has been on the missing persons list for years but was back in the harness long ago.

Probably the largest source of over-reported disappearees are juveniles. In fact, teenage runaways make up such a large proportion of officially missing persons that most MPB's are part of the juvenile section of the police department. It is not uncommon for teenagers to flee unhappy homes or strike out on their own in search of fame and fortune. Even though their parents may have started out the same way, they are quick to report Junior's disappearance to the MPB.

The not-so-amazing fact about teenage runaways is that they seem to find their way home as soon as the money runs out. If Mom & Dad forget to notify the authorities it could be a long time before Junior is stricken from the rolls of the missing. And if the parents move around a lot (especially common with military personnel), their child may be listed as missing in several cities even though he's always come back home. In such a case it is unlikely the MPB's in those cities would ever learn the child's fate or be able to strike him from their records.

Teenage runaways do not fit into the scope of this book because they seldom change identities. They are young and it is relatively easy for them to establish new lives once they reach their destinations. They are not encumbered with the problems and established lives that require adult runaways to build completely new identities. In fact, most teenage runaways re-establish their family ties somewhere down the road.

One of the interesting aspects of teenage runaways is that they often possess the skills and background to become successful adult runaways. They have severed their emotional family ties early in life while developing the skills to survive as "strangers in strange lands." Successful identity-changing later in life will be much easier for these kids than it is for the run-of-the-mill estranged spouse.

The foregoing are only a few of the many reasons for the inaccuracy of missing persons statistics. Some others: people who are murdered but whose bodies are never discovered; people who die without identification, particularly when they are some distance from home;

people killed while posing as someone else. Many people who die in airplane crashes and shipwrecks are never identified or incorrectly identitied.

WHY PEOPLE DISAPPEAR

Now that we have examined *who* disappears, we will try to understand *why* they do it. What motivates reasonable people to take the severe, difficult and often painful act of complete detachment?

Through my encounters with the disappeared I have found three major motivations for the decision: legal, financial and psychological. While some of the cases described below fall neatly into just one of these categories, most people who disappear are motivated by a formula combining all three.

By far the strongest motivation for disappearing is psychological. There are many ways to deal with life's difficult situations without disappearing. Most people fight to overcome their problems through the use of marriage counselors, attorneys, accountants, etc. When they lose, most people do their time, whether in prison or an unhappy marriage. Those who disappear are neither willing to do their time or to battle for something that's not worth the fight.

Generally speaking, deliberate disappearance is a defensive reaction to overwhelming and intolerable social pressures. Furthermore, successful identity change takes a special kind of psyche. Many of those who attempt disappearance are unable to cope with the stark reality of displacement or with the longing for reunion. They find that it's easier to deal with the problems of home than the problems of not having a home. The successful disappearee usually has a taste for risk, the ability to think and act quickly, and either a strong resistance to, or fear of, re-connecting with their past.

Let's look at some of the specific reasons that compel people to abandon their former lives and create new identities for themselves.

Marriage, Divorce & Revenge

As mentioned earlier, the prime reason for disappearing is an unhappy marriage. Men and women caught in an unhappy relationship often dream about leaving their partner and everything else behind and starting over in a new town with a new name. Fear of the unknown and lack of knowledge about identity changing prevents most of them from acting on their wishes. They may even take off one day, but a few nights in boxcars brings them back or they fail to disguise their identity or location and are forcibly brought back. They do not have the psyche of the identity-changer.

For a rare few individuals, the dreams of leaving their spouse eventually develop into concrete plans and a successful escape. I met such a person one evening at Specs' 12 Adler Place Saloon in San Francisco. He recounted his story over a Green Death using the transparent guise of his "friend," a convention I had become familiar with already.

"This friend of mine was in his mid-forties when he decided he'd had enough of his wife. They had been married for many years but never had any children. He had a job that paid him pretty well but was dog-ass boring. About the only thing that meant anything to this guy was model trains. He belonged to a 'model railroaders club' and spent most of his evenings building these complicated models in his basement.

"His pride and joy in life was this elaborate scale model of a High Sierra logging railroad. You should've seen it. He built it all with his own hands and it was the envy of the club. There were articles about it in model-builder magazines and even a feature spread in the local paper.

"One evening his wife followed him downstairs after supper. A man's got to have a private place, you know, to be by himself and that basement was his private place. She shouldn't have gone down there. She was all uptight because he wouldn't go visit her folks with her. She started bitchin' and naggin' and working herself up into a tirade. And what do you think she said to him? 'You think more of that damned toy train set than you do of me.'

"There was something about her tone of voice when she said 'that damned toy train set' that made the light go on. I guess he suddenly realized that she was right, he did care more about his models than he did about her — a helluva lot more! And he knew that this was about as sad a commentary as it's possible to make about the relationship between a man and woman."

"So he split right then and there," I offered.

"No, not just then. She stomped off saying, 'If you want to talk to me, you can reach me at Mother's.' Can you imagine that, a woman of thirty-nine going off to her mother's house?

"He just sat there for a while thinking about what she said and how miserable his life was. Something inside of him clicked and he knew he couldn't take it anymore. He got up, went out to the garage and got a sledge hammer, came back and smashed that model train set-up to pieces! That night he got his things together and moved out. He hasn't set foot in that house since."

"Then what happened?" I asked.

"Well, he cleaned out their bank account the next day. He figured he'd leave her the house, which was almost paid for, and that ought to be good enough for the damn little satisfaction she had given him over the years. The next thing he knew he was ass-deep in legal talent, both hers and his. She was going to divorce him and it looked like she could force him to continue making the house payments. He could have afforded everything because his job paid so well, but then came the straw that broke the camel's back: she sent *him* the bill from a photographer she hired to take pictures of the wrecked model trains to prove to the court that *he* was 'mentally unstable' and had 'violent tendencies.'

"Shortly after that he was sitting in a bar thinking about these goings-on and brooding about the whole mess when he saw an article in the paper about this guy who stepped out for a pack of cigarettes one day and vanished into thin air. He started thinking about his life and realized he didn't have anything to hold him down. He didn't have any emotional ties, he didn't give a shit for his job, he had some money put away, and he was in pretty good health."

"So he took off, just like that guy in the paper," I said.

"Not immediately. He thought about where he would go. He always liked the San Francisco area and so he took a few trips up there. The more he saw, the better he liked it. And the longer he waited, the more he realized that his ex-wife and those ambulance chasers were going to gnaw on his bank account until it was all gone. He went on this way for four or five weeks until he realized that every time he thought about splitting, he felt better. So he did it."

"With no references or ID he must have had a tough time making the switch," I said. I was hoping he'd tell me about rigging-up this new identity, but he looked at me sort of funny as if he'd just realized he had maybe said more than he intended to. He looked over my shoulder and saw something that made him climb off his stool.

"A friend I'm taking out to dinner just arrived," he said. "Thanks for the beer, but I've gotta go. Good luck with your book."

The friend he was meeting was an attractive, well-dressed lady in her late twenties or early thirties. They greeted each other with obvious affection. They chatted, looking over at me a couple times, then left. I've seen neither of them since.

While it is fairly common for a man to leave his wife and disappear, especially if he is being taken to the cleaners in a divorce, it is very rare for a woman to leave her husband. Some of the reasons for this are obvious.

The system of "justice" in the United States is heavily slanted in favor of women in a divorce. Why would a woman want to split on her husband if she could divorce him and make him take care of most of her bills? It wouldn't make any sense.

Also, a woman does not face the same kind of pressures when married as the husband does. Both of them may work, but the man's income and career are usually seen as the financial foundation of the family. And men have more psychological pressures on them to succeed and build a career than women do. A husband usually will not disappear if his marriage turns sour or he hates his job, but the combination of the two can be devastating.

Without a doubt the greatest reason for women to disappear is battering. When a spouse or lover is violently abusive, divorce and separation are not very attractive remedies. In either situation, the estranged woman is still vulnerable while living in the same town or using her real name. The police are unable and, in many cases, unwilling to provide her with adequate protection. In these cases, disappearing may be a matter of basic survival.

Disappearing is further complicated for women who have children. It is hard enough for one person trying to disappear — it is damn near impossible for a whole family to vanish. A woman on her own is not likely to take much abuse before walking out on her man; women with children have been known to put up with an awful lot before seeking help. And the longer the woman puts up with it, the more likely her man is to hunt her down if she tries to leave.

It is the fear of being harmed that is the cause of most female identity changes. Perhaps this is why I have never talked with a woman disappearee. A man who successfully adopts a new identity is justifiably proud of his achievement and is willing to talk about it with a perfect stranger. But a woman who has disappeared out of fear for her safety is not likely to reveal her secret to anyone she hasn't come to know intimately.

Occasionally, the deciding factor that makes a husband disappear is a desire for revenge. The abandoned wife is, in almost all respects, in a far worse position than a widow. All her alternatives will be expensive and difficult, including hiring detectives to find him, getting a divorce or having him declared legally dead. And she is not likely to have many resources at her disposal to pay for these things.

In most cases it will be a year or longer before she can sell any real or personal property that's in his name or in both of their names. Depending on where she lives she may not be able to sell property in her own name immediately. In the meantime, she will have to make all the payments due on the property, yet she will have to have a court action to use any monies due her husband, such as wages, tax returns, etc. Chances are he collected what he had coming before he split.

If she wants to get married again, she will have to either divorce her spouse or have him declared legally dead. Most women choose the former because it is less time consuming and less expensive. Obtaining a divorce under these circumstances can present severe financial problems, though, especially if the wife was figuring to saddle her ex-husband with the tab. Lawyers understand this situation and are prone to requesting fees up-front.

If the wife wants to collect on her husband's life insurance policy, she will have to get him declared legally dead. The procedures for getting such a declaration vary greatly from state to state and the whole process can be

13

blocked by a particularly malicious husband. I know of one case where a husband penned a note on the datelined front page of a newspaper, then mailed the note to his life insurance company. Needless to say, the insurance company refused to pay off on the substantial policy.

Dual Identities & Lovers

I once met a cheerful bigamist at the Operating Engineers hiring hall in San Mateo, California. This enterprising fellow had two wives, two families and two identities and divided his time evenly between them. He worked on construction jobs during the summer and repaired ski lifts during the winter. When the snow was thick on the ground he was drawing tax-free unemployment based on his previous summer's work, and during the hot months he drew benefits based on his winter job. Both his wives had jobs paying above-the-norm salaries, so the dual-family set-up was not a drain on him financially.

This information was elicited in the course of a casual conversation, but when I began asking specific and probing questions such as, "How did you work yourself into this situation in the first place?" and "Do your wives know each other?" I overstepped the boundaries of his privacy and he clammed up, turned on his heels and left. I've wondered for years whether he will carry these arrangements into retirement and reap Social Security benefits from both identities...

Contrary to widely-held opinion, the "other woman" is seldom a serious factor in most decisions to effect a deliberate disappearance, and it is rare for a man to disappear and take his "sidelines lover" with him. This is probably due to the practical reason that engineering the disappearance of two people is vastly more complicated than one. One of the basic attributes of a person willing and able to disappear and create a new identity is rock-ribbed practicality.

Boredom & Frustration

There is something about the middle years of life, the forties to fifties, that makes a man take a long, hard look at himself, his works, and his future. For then it is that he comes face-to-face with the ashes of his dreams and realizes that he is most definitely not going to write the Great American Novel. Or become President of The Company. Or even A MultiMillionaire.

The great majority of men pass through this stage by simply gritting their teeth and continuing right on schlepping. A very, very few become so depressed they commit suicide. A larger number, also profoundly discouraged, commit the "revocable suicide" and disappear with the thought that they will leave their troubles behind. Sometimes it works.

The "social scientists" call this the "Gauguin Syndrome" after the French stockbroker who chucked it all to paint and contract syphilis in the South Sea Islands. In the interests of accuracy, Gauguin did not change his identity — only his lifestyle and goals. He was really a run-of-the-mill dropout, not a disappearee.

One slow evening in the bar at the Old Shasta Royal Lodge above Dunsmuir, California, I was idling away the time in casual conversation with a traveler who had taken a room for the night. My companion, a well-turned-out man of about fifty, became avidly interested when I mentioned I was researching a book about the techniques of disappearances. When the conversation came around to the reasons for disappearing, he said musingly, "You know, the situation that a very near friend of mine found himself in may be of interest to you."

Naturally I made all the appropriate noises and he continued with his story.

"My friend was married to a small-town New England girl. Together they had raised three fine children. He worked as a teacher for a small school system on the

15

Cape, which was fine enough when he started. After seven years he established tenure, but the pay was barely enough to make ends meet. He noticed that more and more he had a feeling of being trapped; he was bored and dissatisfied with his job, but with four mouths to feed he didn't dare give up his tenured position for a job at some other school, and other high-paying jobs are hard to come by in resort areas like the Cape.

"He and his wife began to squabble about their finances. As the kids got older the debts started to pile up. In order to pay the bills and keep peace in the family, he took a summer job as a pump jockey at a nearby gas station. Can you imagine the humiliation of a forty-year-old man pumping gas, or the anger that grew inside him every time a neighbor or colleague pulled in for a fill-up? It became unbearable."

He paused, realizing that his emotion recounting these events was giving away the true identity of his "friend." I could see he was debating whether to continue so I prompted him to get to the heart of the story.

"It doesn't sound to me like your friend could last very long in a situation like that," I said, reestablishing the pretense of the "friend."

"You're right about that. A man will sacrifice a lot for his family, but when he gives up his pride and dignity he becomes something less than a man. Even with the extra cash, matters got worse at home, the fights became more frequent, his marriage became miserable and intolerable. Every time he looked at his wife he was reminded of the dreams he had set aside for her sake. Eventually the price he was paying didn't seem worth the relationship and they decided to divorce.

"His wife got the house, the car and custody of the kids. Suddenly my friend realized he had absolutely nothing to show for his years of hard work. He got stuck paying alimony and child support, which meant he had to keep both jobs and continue working through his summers. That summer vacation was about the only thing he enjoyed about his teaching job and now that was gone like everything else.

"The final blow was a bill from the orthodontist for *fifteen hundred dollars.* His wife was obviously out to get as much as she could out of him before the kids became legal adults and the child-support ended. That bill would have wiped out the meager savings he had been able to put aside. He called his lawyer who advised him to pay the bill. He could fight it out in court but he would end up paying both the bill and his attorney's fees and court costs. My friend got so depressed he seriously contemplated suicide.

"What probably saved him was an article he remembered reading about a man in Providence who was in similar straits and simply walked out one evening and never returned. He took a hard look at his life and recognized that everything he had worked for was gone along with his enthusiasm for the future. He loved his kids, but they would soon be adults building lives of their own. He wouldn't have even considered disappearing if his children were still at that youthful stage where they need to have a father around. So he rounded up all the cash he could get his hands on and hopped on a bus for Boston late one summer night, and he's never looked back."

"Have you seen your friend since he disappeared?" I asked. "I wonder if he had any regrets."

"Yes, I'm still in touch with my friend," he said, with a smile exchanged between those who hold a secret, "and he has had regrets, of course. He misses his kids terribly. But he figures his wife got enough out of the divorce to take care of the kids until they're old enough to start their own careers. And as for his wife, hell, it might do her some good to have to work for a living. Maybe she'll understand the kind of pressures that finally got to her husband.

17

"As for my friend's new life, it couldn't be better. He's not a teacher anymore, nor a gas station attendant. Let's say he found a job far more interesting than he ever imagined he could get. And he's with a wonderful woman now who earns her own keep, to boot. Yes, even though he has some regrets, they are far outweighed by the fantastic improvement in the quality of his life."

Social Security

A surprisingly large number of "retired" people establish a second identity so they can work and still draw their maximum Social Security benefits. They feel they have paid into their account all their lives and they are entitled to a pension just as they would be entitled to an annuity that has been bought and paid for. They cannot see the logic in the law's reducing their benefits if they continue to work. So they devise another identity, obtain a second Social Security number, and re-enter the ranks of the employed on a *sub-rosa* basis.

Although the instances of using a second identity to defeat the inequitable Social Security system are many — in fact, a helluva lot more than the S.S.A. would care to think about — ordinarily a disappearance is not involved. I mention these cases here only because they usually involve a well-thought-out identity invention together with painstaking documentation.

On the Lam & In the Slammer

A great number of disappearees are suspected or convicted criminals engaged in unlawful flight to avoid prosecution. Criminals, like the battered women discussed earlier, are very reluctant to discuss their stories with strangers. Indeed, I did not hear any true

18

criminal disappearance stories during my research for this book. This is not surprising, considering that it is the criminal identity-changer's insistence on absolute privacy that keeps him out of the clutches of the law. A jilted spouse will usually give up a difficult hunt, but the feds never stop.

With the exception of paperhangers, embezzlers, con men and similar white-collar-type criminals, most lawbreakers do not plan their disappearances well enough to evade a determined police effort to apprehend them. Every day one reads about some wanted man being picked up in his girl friend's apartment or even at his mother's house — the very last places in the world he has any business being!

A perfect example of this ineptness was the convict in a Michigan slammer whose friends sprung him with an elaborate helicopter caper, a la the movie *Breakout*. Instead of putting considerable distance between himself and the high stone walls the moment he was sprung, he proceeded to enjoy the finer things of life in the local watering holes. The cops wound up arresting him in a gin mill about fifteen miles from the main gate. He was free a total of one week.

One unique attribute of criminal disappearees is that they tend to get better with practice. Middle-class husbands who duck out on their wives' attorneys are rarely ever located but criminals on the run are often brought back time and again. After their first or second re-arrest they begin to understand what it takes to stay free and they plan very carefully for their next foray into the free world. The seasoned identity changer is probably the most difficult disappearee to locate.

A very few of the people who disappear and change their identities are serving time and don't want their friends or relations to know about it. In this light it is interesting to note that a man can do his stretch under any name he chooses provided the authorities can't make a positive identification. Although the identity change is genuine, the disappearance would have to come under the heading "involuntary" and hence is beyond the scope of this book.

Amnesia

Genuine amnesia is extremely rare, not nearly as common as one would be led to believe by TV and newspapers, and even rarer as a factor in a prolonged disappearance and identity change. The true amnesiac is often badly confused and either seeks help or is picked up by the police because he is unable to care for himself. It is not so rare, however, for a disappearee to *plead* amnesia upon returning to the family fold. And the family readily accepts this flimsy explanation because it is a convenient way out of a situation embarrassing to all concerned.

Rebellion & Adventure

Although I talked to no disappearee who vanished as a gesture of rebellion against "the system" per se, many of the respondents had nothing but contempt for the maze of forms and petty regulations used by business and government to control the masses. I found it amusing that their contempt stemmed from the fact that they found the vaunted controls so easy to subvert.

One man I spoke with was perfectly confident that he could disappear successfully because back in WW II he had found it an absolute cinch to con the United States Army into giving him an honorable discharge during his first six months in the service. He resolved to do the deed after a pot-bellied superior gave a speech to the effect that bilking the Army was a physical impossibility and anyone attempting to do so would spend the rest of the war in the stockade. His only regret is that he didn't put enough effort into the charade to wind up with a lifelong, tax-free pension.

Apparently there are a few romantically-inclined individuals who disappear simply for the hell of it. Most of them are probably younger people who would otherwise have no pressing need to go through the considerable trouble of effecting an identity change. The disappearees I talked to were aghast at the very idea of it, taking the attitude that anyone who disappeared for a lark, given the difficulties of establishing and documenting a new identity, ought to have his head examined!

HOW
— THE MECHANICS OF
DISAPPEARING

"An adventure is usually the penalty for lousy planning." **—Shorty Jenkins, Miner & Prospector, Durango, Mexico 1943.**

The way a disappearance is begun usually determines how it will end. The person who blows out one night without any preparation or planning is likely to return soon, either brought back by force or an inability to withstand the rigors of anonymity. On the other hand, the most successful vanishers are those whose disappearance was planned well in advance and painstakingly executed.

Most disappearances fall between the extremes of the careful planner and the spur-of-the-moment drop-out. Many of the disappearances that look on the surface like whimsical undertakings are actually the result of years of detailed and methodical planning *even though the person doing the planning may not actually realize it at the time.* Let me explain this phenomenon.

THE "UNPLANNED" DISAPPEARANCE

One of the more popular and conventional forms of daydreaming, especially for men, is the wishful contemplation of getting away from it all. How many of us would like to chuck the humdrum, boring existence we lead and exchange it for exciting, perhaps dangerous, adventure? The banker may want to be a Northwoods guide, the chemist a cowhand in New Mexico, the chain-store executive a big-time magazine photographer.

Most men have such fantasies but how many ever realize them? Merely hinting at such secret desires earns the dreamer the ridicule of family and peers who scoff at the idea of changing occupations and locations late in the game of life. Spouses may be afraid to take the risks of reducing the family income or leaving a community they have grown comfortable in. Co-workers may find it impossible to imagine such a radical change in lifestyle; their greatest fear may be of the realization that a large and exciting world exists outside the confines of their nine-to-five routine.

And so the dreamer keeps his fantasies to himself. He may buy maps of South America, guidebooks to arctic Alaska, magazines on single-handed boating. He may have these delivered to where he works to keep his family from scoffing at him. He goes on dreaming about the lifestyle of a carefree traveler, but he never breathes a word about it around work or home.

Then one day something happens. Maybe it's a bad argument with his wife about their finances, or he misses out on that promotion he thought was his for sure, and something inside him snaps. That's when he realizes he's gone through this journey a thousand times in his head — why not live it out? What's holding him back now? After dinner one night he goes out for a pack of smokes and never returns. While he never "planned" to disappear, his years of "aimless" dreaming provided him with most of the materials he needed, particularly a mental blueprint of where he would go and what he would do once he got there.

The disappearee who originally piqued my interest in the subject was an example of an unpremeditated disappearance. He realized that it was just fantastic luck that made his disappearance possible. But he had a quick mind and took advantage of the opportunities that arose and enabled him to live *incognito*. His name was "Capa."

Capa

A few years ago I had an assignment to do a magazine article that entailed my going to La Paz, Mexico. As it was Easter Holy Week and all the flights to that part of Mexico were booked, I had to catch a flight to Tucson then take a bus from Nogales, Arizona to Mazatlan where I could catch a ferry to La Paz.

My seatmate on the bus out of Nogales was a quiet, unprepossessing gentleman in his mid-forties who introduced himself as "Capa." What hair he had left was shot with gray and he wore a mustache of a type very common in Mexico but seldom seen in the U.S. since silent movies went out. I was standing behind him in the ticket line in Nogales and was amused that he spoke fluent Central American Spanish with a Southern U.S. accent.

We passed small talk between us as the bus began its long journey. I couldn't help the feeling that something about this fellow was very unusual. For one, he pointedly did not say where he lived or what sort of work he did — two of the first bits of information usually exchanged between travelers. Then there was the name "Capa." It means, among other things, cloak, pretense, mask, cover, that which hides. It is not a common name for someone of Spanish descent.

Then there was the accent. When I casually commented on this he glanced at me sharply and I thought I had offended him. Then he smiled and said, "Thanks, I didn't realize that. Where I live I doubt if anyone would recognize a regional American accent. The information is deeply appreciated. I'll have to watch out for that in the future."

We had a difficult time conversing without having to shout over the two redneck drunks sitting in front of us. They were off on a fishing excursion and passed the time comparing notes on their nagging wives and thinking up schemes for breaking away from their dreary lives. When their conversation turned to disappearing and creating new identities I noticed that Capa, who until now had seemed annoyed at the louts, took a keen interest in their discussion. They concluded this wasn't a practical scheme because of the web of paperwork the U.S. citizen is subjected to. The discussion continued along these lines until they reached Las Mochis and got off the bus.

I was glad to see the drunks depart because it meant that I could hold a civil conversation with Capa, who seemed a most interesting and mysterious man.

As the bus started out of the depot, Capa turned to me and said, "Those drunks were full of shit, you know."

"In what way?" I asked.

"About disappearing and taking on a new identity. It is done all the time in every country of the world, and most countries have much, much more paperwork to contend with than the United States."

He sounded very authoritative on the subject, and I could tell it was of particular interest to him. I thought of the stories I had read in the papers about fugitives who had changed identities to escape the law and how they seemed to always get caught. "I imagine it's a very difficult feat to pull off," I said. "Probably something used only by criminals and the like."

"Not at all," he replied. "It's much easier than you think. A good friend of mine once pulled it off and I don't believe he'll ever be discovered. It is a most interesting story, if you care to hear it."

I told him I did. This was my first encounter with the ubiquitous "friend" I would encounter over and over again while researching this book. What follows is the story he spun as reconstructed from the notes I made in Mazatlan while waiting for the ferry to La Paz.

"I had a friend who lived in one of those textbook examples of a sleepy Southern town that still exist here and there. Let's call him 'Paul,' which is not his real name, of course.

"Paul came from one of the so-called 'leading families' of the South, complete with the bronze statue of an ancestor on the courthouse lawn. He married the daughter of another of the town's 'leading families' — a second cousin, as a matter of fact. They were not really 'in love.' They had married because they were expected to marry. They had two kids who eventually became the only thing holding them together. As time passed, Paul's wife became more involved with establishing herself in local society and Paul escaped more and more into his love of boats.

"Paul and his wife began to argue frequently, and their fights seemed to center around his love of boating. His wife resented his hobby and felt it kept him from participating in the social events she was constantly arranging. She refused to ever join him on his little day sailer. As their quarrels grew more violent he consented to sell the boat to keep peace in the family. From that day forward he kept his hobby sheltered from his wife.

"He continued to read everything he could about boats and single-handing, but the magazines and books now came to his office instead of his home. He taught himself navigation through a mail order course, bought himself a plastic sextant and measured the height of every building, chimney and telephone pole he could see from his office window. But his relationship with his wife only seemed to get worse.

"Then one day the inevitable happened. He began to dream about disappearing, about changing his identity and buying a boat. Then he could spend the rest of his life gunkholing around all the places he'd read about for so many years. Of course, he never had the slightest intention of actually doing it. He had always done the conventional, expected things and could be expected to go on that way for the rest of his natural life.

"One balmy May afternoon Paul took off work early and went down to the river to see if any boats were coming in. It turned out to be a lucky day because there was a sailboat headed into the dock — a rare occurrence on an inland river. Paul hopped out of his car and went over to help the lone sailor tie-up. To his delight, the skipper invited him aboard for a mug-up.

"The skipper was amazed by the fact that Paul knew the proper names and functions of every item on a fairly large sailboat. When Paul mentioned that he'd taught himself navigation the skipper made him an offer. Seems he started out with a mate who got cold feet and left him about halfway down the river. He couldn't handle the boat himself on the open sea, so he asked Paul to accompany him on a 'leisurely cruise down the Caribbean to Yucatan, then down to Panama.'"

"And of course Paul jumped at the chance," I said.

"No. In fact, he didn't even consider it seriously, although it sounded like a marvelous opportunity. No, he went home at the usual hour, but came back to the ketch after dinner for another gam. The skipper stayed docked-up for several days during which Paul spent most of his free hours on board. They grew to be close friends bound by a common affection for sailboats and the sea.

"On the skipper's last night in town Paul had a very depressing dinner conversation with his wife. She didn't appreciate his mysterious late-night rendezvous. She was planning to attend a society ball that evening and she insisted Paul accompany her. He refused, she got hostile, and it ended with Paul ducking out to see his friend off.

"To make a long story short, when the skipper cast off the next morning he had a new mate. Paul had no intention of leaving permanently. He figured he'd ride down the river to New Orleans where the skipper could pick up a new mate. He didn't have his passport and he sure wasn't going out into international waters without it. When they reached New Orleans he explained to the skipper that he'd have to go back home.

"The skipper just grinned like a Cheshire cat. It seems his former mate had forgotten his passport behind a cushion on the settee. They looked it over and, although the picture didn't resemble Paul, the basic statistics were a pretty good match. A few weeks growth of beard and Paul probably wouldn't have any trouble with the immigration officials.

"Paul's world suddenly opened up before his eyes. He knew what he could expect from his wife if he went back home after his brief river ride. On the other hand, here was the opportunity of a lifetime to live out his dreams of sailing through the waters of foreign lands. He could still return home in a couple months, and the reaction from his wife would be no worse than if he went back immediately. So he took the skipper up on his offer and set out for adventure."

"What about the car he left on the dock?" I asked. "I'm sure the police would find it, connect it with the boat, and be after him in no time."

"That's a good question. A few years ago my friend hired a private detective to check up on his family, out of curiosity. Paul had left the keys in the car and it turned up a few months later stripped clean as a jay-bird's ass. After about a year his wife had him declared legally dead and collected on his life insurance. That was easy enough for a woman with her connections, given the discovery of the stripped car and the fact that Paul had never mentioned the idea of disappearing to anyone.

"The minute she got her hands on the money, she married one of her own crowd. I doubt if she would say anything if she happened to meet Paul face-to-face again, which is *very* unlikely, because if the insurance company finds out he's still alive they'll want their money back."

"So I imagine your friend is still out sailing the world then," I said.

"No. This all happened several years ago. And Paul was blessed and cursed by an unusual circumstance. The skipper pulled into a little port in — well, let's just say in a typical Atlantic banana republic port — several months later. While Paul was ashore buying some provisions the skipper had a coronary and fell onto the dock. Needless to say, they don't have the kind of emergency medical services down there that we take for granted. When Paul returned to the boat he found his partner dead on the dock with a crowd of locals standing around.

"The local officials asked Paul to bring the skipper's papers around after *siesta* so they could take care of the formalities. Dazed by the death of his friend and numb with the many beers he had downed since, Paul rummaged through the ship's papers to find the skipper's passport. It wasn't until the local Chief of Police started reading the statistics aloud as he wrote them down that Paul realized he had given the man the wrong passport.

"When Paul realized what he had done he decided not to mention his mistake to the locals. If he had, he would have been on the beach with no money, no job, no working papers and almost no language of the country. But if he let the matter lay he could become the skipper as easily as he adopted the identity of the former mate."

"What happened when the death got reported in the U.S. papers?" I asked. "I would imagine that Paul's plans would fall apart if there was an investigation."

"Paul had several things going for him in this respect. Because the death didn't involve a famous or noteworthy person, it probably never got mentioned anywhere except the local Spanish-language newspaper. Since there was obviously no foul-play involved the police never made a formal investigation of the death. And a U.S. passport with several years still to run on it is worth a fair amount on the black market down there. I imagine the Chief of Police never got around to sending it back to the U.S."

"So where is Paul today?" I asked.

"Well, he sold the ketch after about six months more on the seas. He'd lived out his sailing dreams and he was getting anxious to rejoin the civilized world. He had plenty of time to think about his new identity and the options available to him. He took the proceeds from the sale of the boat and went into business in one of the Central American countries. He's done quite well there. In fact, he's engaged to the only daughter of one of the Catorce." ("Catorce" means "fourteen" in Spanish and in Central America refers to the fourteen families that are rumored to own and operate El Salvador. — Ed.)

"I imagine he'd be under pretty close scrutiny there," I said. "Those people are very likely to investigate any gringo who's going to marry into their family."

Capa gave a broad grin. "Investigate they did, though he's not supposed to know it. They found out the skipper was Catholic, had been a widow for ten years, and had been a respectable, successful businessman who was well thought of by all who knew him in his home town."

After he finished Paul's story, Capa quizzed me about the San Francisco Bay Area. He said he'd read a lot about it and hoped to visit there in the not-too-distant future.

I was in Sausalito a few months later photographing a houseboat story for *Rudder* magazine when I heard someone calling my name. I turned to see Capa, smiling broadly, with a very attractive young woman hanging on his arm. We repaired to The Bar With No Name for a few bottles of Anchor Steam Beer.

It turned out that Capa was honeymooning with his new Central American bride. She was a charming young lady with all the outward marks of old money and expensive schooling. I'd guess her age to be about twenty to twenty-five years, about twenty years younger than her new husband.

As we were making our farewells on the sidewalk in front of the bar, I couldn't resist a mild parting shot. "Looks to me as if your friend Paul you told me about on the bus is doing a lot better nowadays than he was back in the Bible Belt."

Capa's teeth flashed in his sun-browned face and he half-bowed, his young lady waved, and they were gone.

PLANNING TO DISAPPEAR

Capa's story of his friend "Paul" is an example of the "unplanned" disappearance. Paul had several things going for him. First, he had spent years studying boats, sailing and the geography of the places he wanted to visit. When he took off, he had the skills and knowledge to successfully travel by water. Second, he was lucky enough to fall into a new identity. And third, the time he spent at sea allowed him to grow into his new identity without having to immediately find a job or a place to live.

Most disappearances start out the same way as Paul's did. People dream of more exotic lifestyles and collect books, magazines, maps, even equipment, but they rarely put their knowledge and tools to use by practicing hiking, boating, photography, or whatever. And they never even seriously consider discarding their identity, or contemplate the difficulties they would face building a new one.

Unlike Paul, however, when that fateful day of the lost promotion or ugly family squabble hits, these dreamers don't just take off on a boat and leave their troubles behind. Once they realize they can no longer live the way they have been, their adventurous dreams turn into hardcore planning. They start to assemble fake ID. They research the mechanics of identity change. They study the bureaucratic requirements of city, state and federal governments, of foreign nations and employers. They *prepare* their disappearance.

A funny thing happens when these dreamers suddenly become planners. They have more or less made the decision to leave and it is like a great weight is lifted from their shoulders. Their work and family life become more bearable. Things seem to be improving for them. But it is only the calm before the storm. One day they wake up and decide that this is going to be the *last* day, and they walk out the front door into a whole new life they've prepared.

The comparison between suicide and identity change is an interesting one. In both cases the person feels driven to the act as a solution to his problems. He is depressed and irritable until he seizes on the "final solution," and then his burdens seem lighter and his mood picks up. This could account for how surprised people are when someone commits suicide. How often have you heard the relatives of a suicide victim tell a reporter, "I can't understand why John would want to kill himself. We might have understood it better a few months ago when he was so upset about his life, but he has been so happy lately. It doesn't make sense."

Disappearing is a form of suicide. It is a revocable kind of death where one destroys his old life but not his chance to start a new one. If the new life doesn't work out as planned he can step back into his old one, though it probably won't be the same. If he's gone very long, he may never be able to regain his family or his job. That's why most disappearees who are gone more than a few weeks never return unless they're fugitives who are hunted down and brought back by the law.

It is fairly common for people who disappear to want to make their escape look like a suicide. They could probably just as easily walk out the door into a new identity, but for some reason they want people to think they have died. Perhaps they believe it will keep people from searching for them, or that it will be easier for their families to cope with death than with disappearance. Then again, it may be a scam to collect on life insurance. Dr. Richard Seiden of the University of California, an internationally known authority on suicide, has coined a new word for such fake deaths: Pseudocide.

Pseudocide

Dr. Seiden investigated 100 cases of apparent suicide from the Golden Gate Bridge in which no body was recovered. Of the 100, he easily found 26 that were alive and well and enjoying the finer side of life. His investigative techniques were not very sophisticated either, so it is likely that many of the remaining 74 "victims" are out walking the streets somewhere.

The very first suicide from the San Francisco Bay Bridge was actually a pseudocide. The person in question was a San Francisco Supervisor, similar to a councilman or alderman, who was embroiled in a little dispute with the accounting types over the disposal of some official funds. When the situation got serious he took the easy way out and was written off the books as a bridge suicide even though his remains were never located. Sometime later he was discovered selling bibles door-to-door down in Texas.

I heard about another pseudocide through one of my phone contacts. A young fellow who had suffered as much of his wife and job as he could handle decided the best alternative was to bow out of that life forever. He spent

33

months accumulating documents, planning for his new life, and hatching an elaborate plan for disappearing. In all this he was aided by a close buddy, which is very unusual. Most disappearees go it alone.

The disappearee left his house late one night in his car to meet his friend. His friend had borrowed his sister's car, which was registered in the name of his brother-in-law. To go with the borrowed car, the friend had a fake driver's license using his brother-in-law's name with his own photograph. The two of them drove their cars to a nearby bridge. I believe it was the Golden Gate, though the caller wouldn't identify the bridge.

It was a foggy night and visibility on the bridge was almost nil. The disappearee-in-the-making pulled up along the curb at the middle of the bridge, laid his billfold on the seat, then joined his friend who had pulled-up slightly in front of him. Together they flagged down a passing motorist, telling the driver that they had seen someone jump off the bridge but they couldn't get to him in time to stop him. They asked the motorist to go phone the police while they waited at the scene.

The disappearee had planned his deed well. The billfold he left on the seat was absent any picture identification of the supposed jumper, though there were plenty of pictures of his wife and relatives and a lot of non-picture ID. When the police arrived, they told them the story. The police took down their names; the disappearee had a complete set of fake ID already assembled for his new identity and his friend used his brother-in-law's name and ID.

The police accepted the story at face value, and why not? Bridge suicides are not uncommon, but witnesses to them are rare. Here the police had two sober, reliable-looking witnesses. There was never a thorough investigation made and as no body was found there wasn't a coroner's inquest which would have required the witnesses to appear in court. The incident was listed officially as a suicide and the young disappearee left the scene feeling like "a new man."

As clever as this pseudocide was, I believe that a serious identity changer would forgo the fake-death routine for an out-and-out disappearance. Our young bridge-jumper has taken a number of unnecessary risks. For one, his new name is now in official police files and is tied-in with his old identity. What if his "ex"-wife wanted to speak with the witnesses herself? Also, both of the witnesses' names might well appear in a newspaper police-beat column. Think of the surprise of the disappearee's friend's brother-in-law as he read his name in the paper as a witness to a suicide. He might consider it just a coincidence of identical names. Then again, the license number of the brother-in-law's car is likely in the police file, too. What if the wife, unable to track down the witness that was in fact her husband, used the name and license plate of the other witness to track him down? She might be very suspicious if the brother-in-law swears he lent his car that night to a man she knows was her husband's best friend.

If the bridge-jumper had a life insurance policy, chances are they would investigate even if the police didn't. Insurance companies are all-too-familiar with the phony bridge suicide routine, as they have uncovered quite a few not-very-intelligent frauds by people who hoped to use their own life insurance proceeds to get themselves out of debt. With the information contained in the police report the insurance investigators would probably have enough grounds to withhold payment even if they couldn't find the disappearee.

The greatest mistake of our bridge-jumping friend was involving someone else in his plans. One of the ground rules of successful identity change is to keep your plans to yourself. The friend who so freely helps you execute your plans may not be able to withstand the pressures exerted by relatives or the police to locate the missing person.

Your friend may help you destroy *your* old life but doesn't want to see your scheme destroy *his* life. And you won't be there to hold his hand as the police try to coerce your whereabouts out of him.

Do It Alone

Successful identity changers keep their plans to themselves. Further, they rarely take anyone with them when they go. Regardless of what you read in the tabloids, it is very unusual for a man to take his mistress with him into his new life. Of course, women often run off with men and change their names, whether they get married or not. But this does not constitute a disappearance and identity change in the context of this book. It is very difficult for a person to successfully change identities alone. It is damn near impossible to do it in tandem.

Children pose a somewhat different problem. Every now and then the mass media have a heyday with the case of a father who "kidnaps" his own children, removing them from the lawful custody of their mother and the jurisdiction of the local courts. While this makes for entertaining reading, it is highly difficult for a father to place beyond-school-starting-age children in a school for the first time without leaving a paper trail back to their original homes and identities.

Money

Although many disappearees leave with little or no money in their pockets, this is most emphatically doing it the hard way. A financial cushion is a great boon to the lamster. A new identity is a very fragile and delicate thing while it is being established. Like any kind of lie, it can be quickly unraveled if it isn't well thought out. A cash reserve allows a little breathing spell in which to get used to the new identity.

If a man is flat broke when he disappears he is going to face some serious hurdles. Where will he live? If he turns to friends or relatives he risks being caught *and* leaving an easy trail by which to find him. If he sleeps in boxcars and under bridges he greatly increases his chances of an undesirable run-in with the law. How will he get money? He may have a difficult time finding a job if he hasn't been able to document his new identity. Even if he has documentation, careful scrutiny by a personnel department can lead to disaster for someone who hasn't built confidence in his new identity. And if he turns to crime to survive, we're back to the police again.

Identification

Identification is the key to establishing a new identity. Unless you are going to live like a wild man in the woods you are going to need some ID, and even then it couldn't hurt. The disappearee is somewhat aided here by the fixation in the modern world for paperwork. It isn't *who* you are that counts, *but whether you can prove it!* Most disappearees do not find it necessary to disguise their appearance or even change their lifestyles. So long as they can manipulate their paper identity they have very little chance of being discovered.

There is a whole chapter of this book devoted to establishing ID, so I won't go into great detail here, except to say that it is important to consider ID *before* making a break for it. It can take months for even a quick operator to put together a complete set of identification, and this under relatively ideal circumstances of having a stable residence and a confidential mailing address. After all, if you're planning to disappear you don't want the whole world to know you're collecting false identification. You don't want to find yourself in a situation where you need to get your hands on some ID fast. It's best to have your new identity set up in advance even if you will quickly shed your first identity for yet another one.

Mail Drops

As suggested above, one of the first things you should consider when contemplating disappearing is getting a confidential mailing address. You will likely want to get information about identity changing, like this book, that you don't want other people to know about. You'll also need the address for getting fake ID. And you may want to send some assets from your former life ahead of you into your new life. There are several ways to get such an address.

The first, and perhaps best way, is to rent an address. People and businesses all over the globe will sell you the use of their address for a nominal fee. These services are known as *mail drops*. It works like this: for a fee, someone will allow you to use their address for sending and receiving mail. Along with this basic service, mail drops provide a variety of extras. You can arrange to have them forward the mail you receive, or open certain mail on your instructions, or destroy mail, etc. They will also re-mail materials according to your instructions. For more information about how mail drops work and addresses and fees of mail drops, see the *Directory of Mail Drops in the U.S. and Canada*, listed in the reference chapter.

If your needs involve more than the services of a typical mail drop you may want to check on the huge number of enterprises in any large city that rent desk space, telephone service, secretarial service, etc. These firms cater to salesmen, construction workers, photographers, and other people with one-man businesses who need to have the appearance of a full-time office and staff. You can use their address as your business or residence address and hire them to handle phone calls and mail according to your instructions. Such services are especially handy when combined with mail drops for fabricating references on employment applications. More on this subject in the chapter on Coping.

Cars

It is amazing the number of people who take their cars with them when they disappear. When they do, it makes the Missing Persons Bureau's job so very, very easy. All they have to do is wait until the current license or registration expires, then get their information from the renewal or switch. Whether you sell it, swap it or ditch it, your car will be a very valuable and readily discovered clue to your new location and identity.

I interviewed one man who had taken off with his car but had no intention of allowing it to lead to his discovery. The car was a brand new, expensive model that had become the bone of contention between him and his wife. He grew to detest the car almost as much as he loathed her. When he left, he took the car with him halfway across the country.

He then located an auto wrecking yard on the outskirts of a small Midwestern metropolitan area where the employees stripped the car of any re-sellable items that couldn't be directly identified as having come from this specific car. He had all the legal papers to prove that he was at least co-owner of the car, so the owner of the yard had no objection to carrying out the man's request. The man then donated the parts to the yard in exchange for them not making an issue out of the paperwork that is supposed to go to the Department of Motor Vehicles in such cases. He also got a much more gratifying form of compensation than money: they let him watch as they "baled" the car, picking it up with a large, four-pronged claw, then dropping it into a machine that folded it and squeezed it into an unrecognizable cube of scrap metal.

Most disappearees who take their cars with them, however, sell them to work up a little extra cash. This inevitably leaves a paper trail that could in turn lead to their discovery and/or apprehension. It is best to forget the car and use public transportation to effect your escape.

Leaving the Country

A well-planned disappearance should not involve immediately leaving the country unless one has a complete set of U.S. identification papers in the new identity. The majority of foreign countries require a passport or birth certificate and supplemental ID — drivers license, credit cards, other licenses, etc. — from U.S. citizens. Further, these regulations are subject to change from time to time, often *without prior notice.*

As a practical matter, unless one has the proper documentation he is not allowed to board an international flight or a ship bound for a foreign port. If the individual does not have the correct papers, the carrier will be unable to land him at his destination and may be liable for a number of expensive fines. It is advisable to have a passport when traveling anywhere outside the U.S., even to Canada and Mexico where it may not be a legal requirement.

Mexico

As I have spent a considerable amount of time traveling "south of the border," it might help to clear up a few popular misconceptions about Mexico. The published information on Mexican *migracion* regulations gives the picture as it's supposed to be, not as it really is.

According to the articles in the Sunday Paper travel section, Mexico requires a birth certificate, passport or other positive means of identification from U.S. citizens before they will be allowed to enter the Republic. Actually, the Mexicans think it is nice if the Yankee *turista* has a birth certificate and/or all those other good things, but they aren't going to refuse admission to a potential contributor to their shaky economy just because he's short a piece of paper. Not too many U.S. citizens travel with their birth certificates and most of them don't even *have* a passport!

What Mexico actually demands is "proof" of nationality. Drivers licenses and a lot of other things are acceptable. And Mexican rules provide for issuing tourist permits even in the absence of these things, and allow the immigration officials to charge a small fee (about $25 U.S. the last time I heard) or not, as they see fit. Or they may refuse entry altogether. If this situation occurs, a small *propina* is definitely in order, say in the neighborhood of $5 to $10 U.S.

This is a good place to explain the often misunderstood difference between a *"propina"* and the infamous *"mordita"*. A *propina* is a gratuity, freely offered and usually readily accepted. You leave a *propina* for the waitress or the guy who washes your car. In the example above, the $5 offered the immigration official is a *propina*, but if he turns it down and demands $50, it becomes a *mordita* pure and simple.

When dealing with Mexican border officials, the rule regarding *propinas* is "don't overdo it!" If you give $50 when $5 is more in order the official may wonder at the reason for your generosity. He knows if he can get $50 without asking he stands a mighty good chance to boost the ante by taking you down to the *carcel* and bouncing you around a little.

Nearly all magazine articles on Mexico emphasize the "fact" that a single parent taking his child or children into Mexico must have notarized permission from the other

41

parent before they will be admitted. It just ain't so in my own experience traveling in the Republic with minor children. Sometimes a woman is hassled a little, but even this is not too common. A small *propina* helps at times, but is seldom obligatory.

The ordinary tourist permit is issued for 180 days, although it is often issued for lesser periods. When the permit expires, Mexican law states that it must be renewed at the border or at a Mexican Consulate. This is why it is common at ports of entry to see expatriate Yanks walk across the border, turn around and head back into the Republic.

Theoretically it is possible for a foreigner to become a full citizen of Mexico, but practically it is impossible. I have met people who have been trying for 30 years to get their Mexican citizenship but were always thwarted at the very last instant by some minute, invisible defect in their paperwork. For what it's worth, the easiest way to become a citizen of the Republic is to get yourself born there. In some cases, this can be accomplished "after the fact" through a small donation to some official's "favorite charity," or by having the right friends.

Now that I've discussed getting into Mexico, I'll add that for most Americans, Canadians or other foreigners, Mexico is a lousy haven. For one thing, it is difficult if not impossible for a foreigner to get work there. Mexico is an extremely xenophobic country, which is to say they believe in "Mexico for the Mexicans," and don't want U.S. citizens or Costa Ricans or Salvadorans or anyone else coming to their country and making it tough for the locals to get work. The fact that they sometimes act otherwise is because of the necessity of cultivating tourism, which is one of the leading generators of foreign exchange. In all honesty, from the Mexican government's point of view the ideal arrangement would be for foreigners to mail their contributions rather than bringing them along in person.

This is not to deny that many a disappearee from this country has wound up drinking Dos Equis and enjoying the balmy weather back in the Mexican highlands. But most gringos seem to lack the facility to adapt themselves to local customs and mores. The differences between Mexico and the English-speaking world run much deeper than language or etiquette. Living in Mexico is the answer for only a very, very small minority of Yankee disappearees.

WHO'S LOOKING FOR YOU

When preparing a disappearance and identity change, it is best to consider who might be looking for you and the means they are likely to employ trying to find you. One of the best ways to learn this information is to read a book like *How to Find Missing Persons* (see reference chapter) "backwards;" that is, if you know how people will look for you, you'll know what to do and what to avoid doing. I'll give a brief summary here of some of the more likely pursuers.

Missing Persons Bureaus

The person who makes a planned, deliberate disappearance has little to fear in the way of apprehension by the local police department's Missing Persons Bureau (MPB). For starters, the MPB in most police departments is sort of an afterthought, mostly designed to keep anxious relatives out of the desk sergeant's hair and to track down runaway juveniles. The cops aren't likely to put their crack detectives on this beat, to say the least. And because disappearing in and of itself is not a crime, the local police are unlikely to mount an expensive and usually fruitless search.

The MPB will do the routine paperwork, however, and it's surprising just how many people are uncovered through the simplest of investigations. Most of the people the MPB finds did not change their names, much less their identities, and did not leave the local vicinity. Many more are picked up through their automobiles, either from being pulled over for a traffic violation and run through the computer or by having their license and registration traced. Still others are apprehended in flop houses and shelters, the first place the MPB looks — if it looks at all — or are caught for minor crimes like shoplifting or breaking and entering.

The MPB's will almost never find a serious disappearee or identity changer, unless by accident. The U.S. does not have a national police department per se, although it does have the FBI, which will be discussed below. The MPB's will not pursue a disappearee across state lines even if they do share information with other MPB's. You have a good chance of staying undetected as long as you follow the simplest of identity-changing procedures, or unless there is money or crime involved in your disappearance, in which case it won't be the MPB's you have to worry about.

The Feds

Disappearing on your wife is one thing, but fleeing prosecution or taking "French leave" with your employer's money are a different matter altogether. These are cases for the "hard" divisions of the police, including the FBI. These detectives are fairly competent at this kind of work. Some of them are experts. And while the FBI *doesn't* always get their man, they never give up trying. You will have to be very quick and very careful if you disappear to keep out of the clutches of the law.

Larry Lavin knows how persistent and thorough the FBI can be. Reared in Haverhill, Massachusetts, Lavin put

44

himself through the University of Pennsylvania dental school with proceeds from his growing drug distribution business. By the time he graduated he was a millionaire. The police first made contact with Lavin in February of 1983 when a related investigation revealed the size of his unreported income and the FBI suspected it had come from drugs.

Lawrence W. Lavin was indicted in September of 1984, charged with masterminding a cocaine syndicate the FBI agents described as the largest in Philadelphia's history. Before discovering Lavin in 1982, federal authorities suspected that organized crime moved 26 pounds of cocaine into the Philadelphia area every month. Through a taped telephone conversation in 1983, the FBI learned that Lavin's organization was handling 44 pounds of cocaine *a week*. What the feds didn't know was the lengths Lavin would go to avoid prison, or that he began preparing his flight after his initial contact with the FBI in 1983, a full year-and-a-half prior to his indictment. When the FBI moved in on Lavin two days before Halloween in 1984, suspecting that he would jump bail, they found his mansion empty. It would be 18 months before the FBI would get another crack at Lavin.

Once the FBI tipped him off in 1983, Larry Lavin began to prepare for the inevitable. He started working out with weights because he felt a small man like himself would be victimized in prison. He bought a couple books on fake ID and began collecting birth certificates, Social Security cards, drivers licenses and other identification to support himself and his wife, Marcia. As soon as he was indicted in September of 1984, Larry fleshed-out the final elements of his plan to disappear.

Lavin prepared his new identity in keeping with his Irish Catholic background. He became James O'Neil, his wife Susan O'Neil, and his two-year-old son Christopher O'Neil. He inquired at embassies about extradition treaties with various foreign countries knowing that this information would get back to the FBI and they would suspect he intended to flee the country. On the day he and his family packed up a rented car and drove off, a number of his friends flew out of Philadelphia to various locations throughout the country with tickets bought in the Lavins' names. But Lavin had no intention of giving up the comfortable lifestyle he had grown accustomed to.

The Lavins's drove the car they had rented under an assumed name to Virginia Beach, an affluent resort community outside of Norfolk that is popular with retired, highranking federal employees. Within a few months the "O'Neils" purchased an expensive house in a new waterfront development. His wife gave birth to a baby daughter named Tara O'Neil. Lavin bought a yacht and took up fishing and scuba diving. Popular with the neighbors, he told them he had made a fortune selling a computer company he had founded. He invested the money he brought with him through a variety of channels using several identities he had been able to document. By April of 1985, Lavin was so confident of his successful disappearance that he felt safe making limited contact with his former life.

Larry Lavin agreed to let his wife Marcia write a letter to her mother. He instructed her, however, to describe their new-born daughter as a boy, just in case the letter got into the wrong hands. The letter was mailed through a series of mail drops to disguise their real location. Lavin knew the FBI wanted him badly. He was right.

The FBI prosecutes a thousand drug dealers for every one ringleader they catch. Lavin had put the Philadelphia cocaine organization together himself, and the authorities wanted to put him away very badly. FBI agents seized Marcia's letter after getting a warrant to search her mother's house. But Lavin was clever. There was nothing in the letter to give him away. Except ...

Marcia had described in the letter Christopher's third birthday party, held at one of those family pizza parlors where "the bear brought out his birthday cake & sang him a song." Both the agents on the case were family men who had been to such places, but never saw a bear. They contacted Chuck E. Cheese, the national chain of pizza/entertainment parlors. While Chuck E. Cheese never used a bear, they knew of a chain called Showbiz Pizza operated primarily in the South that employed a cuddly mascot named Billy-Bob the Bear.

The FBI agents also learned that Lavin was going to make a prearranged phone call to his close friend, Ken Weidler. Weidler himself was prosecuted for his part in the cocaine ring and had agreed to cooperate with the feds for a lighter sentence. He didn't like helping them, but he knew Larry had studied wiretapping and surveillance techniques and was not likely to stay on the phone long enough to give the police time to trace it. He was wrong.

While they couldn't trace the exact number, the FBI was able to nail down the 804 area code. Within that area code there were only two Showbiz Pizza outlets — one in Lynchburg and one in Virginia Beach. The FBI knew that hundreds of retired agents lived in the Virginia Beach area, so they mailed out letters to all of them, enclosing color photos of Larry and his wife. The letters paid off. One of the retired agents was a neighbor of Lavin's who had been out fishing on Lavin's boat, only he knew him as Brian James O'Neil.

On May 15, 1985, Larry Lavin, alias James O'Neil, was arrested on a Virginia Beach dock as he climbed off a friend's boat after a day of fishing. Lavin was surprised but unemotional. He agreed to cooperate with the police in exchange for freedom for his wife and kids. Larry Lavin has not been sentenced at this writing. Authorities predict it will be at least 20 years before he is a free man again.

Private Eyes & Skip Tracers

You can see that the life of the identity changer is much more difficult when someone has the resources to back up their compulsion to find him. Corporations and wealthy individuals may not turn to the police because they don't want to publicize your disappearance. Whether they inform the authorities or not, they will often hire private detectives to hunt you down.

Where I went to college there was an exceptionally bright student who just vanished one day. He was one of those "boy geniuses" who entered the university in his young teens and had a difficult time adjusting socially. He was very much into the fantasy game *Dungeons & Dragons* to the extent that he used to act it out in the drainage tunnels that criss-crossed beneath the campus. At first it was thought that his disappearance was related to the game.

This is the sort of story that makes for great newspaper copy, of course. The boy's parents were very wealthy. While they notified the police, they also hired a private detective to search for their son. The media played out the drama for weeks with each new effort made by the police. But it was the private eye that finally found the kid in a hospital in Houston and brought him back home. Nothing much came out in the way of his motive for disappearing except that foul play was not involved.

Not too long ago there was a locally celebrated case in San Francisco where a man who was not a U.S. citizen fled with his children to Mexico. There was important money involved on the mother's side, but none on the father's. The man was promptly located by San Francisco's most prominent private eye and the children were returned to San Francisco within a week.

The more money and/or publicity involved in a disappearance, the more intensive and prolonged the search will be. If it's big money, chances are a good detective agency will be after you, or even the federal government. But for the debtor who leaves his creditors in the lurch, the companies involved will probably write off the money or turn the case over to skip tracers.

Professional tracing agencies are usually after people who have not changed their names and they have difficulty finding a person who undergoes a disappearance-with-identity-change. They are relatively systematic in their search for missing heirs, stockholders, alumni and the like and boast in their advertising of "85% success rates." I strongly suspect that most of the remaining 15% are deliberate, systematic disappearees.

All tracers constantly and persistently go through phone books, directories, newspapers and so on. Chances are they will find a man with an unusual last name or a high profile. Those who change their identities, shun publicity and keep their noses clean should have no difficulty evading this kind of low-level search.

The Salvation Army

A little known facet of the search for missing persons is that there are a number of social agencies who undertake to find disappearees. The Salvation Army is the best known of these, and far and away the most efficient. They mostly find missing sons and daughters, relatives who emigrated from the old country and with whom contact has been lost, missing heirs, etc. They are so involved with this work that they even have a periodical devoted to it.

However, the Salvation Army will not undertake an adverse search. That is, they will only act on behalf of a missing person's immediate family or in instances where it would be to the person's benefit to be located. They are comparatively thorough and far-ranging because of their international facilities. But like most tracing organizations, they are primarily concerned with people who are not deliberately concealing their identity and whereabouts.

Insurance Companies

Another example of where big money is involved, thorough searches are more likely, is the life insurance company. All insurance companies as a rule dislike to pay out money under any circumstances. But they dislike paying out big money more than small claims. As most life insurance policies are for $100,000 and up, any death warrants investigation before they will pay up. And this is particularly true where there is no corpse.

Without a cold body you must have the disappearee declared legally dead to collect the life insurance. The life insurance companies do not have to find the person to withhold payment. All they must do is prove that he is alive and healthy somewhere. With the kind of financial incentives involved, insurance companies are likely to mount a much more intensive search than the local Missing Persons Bureau.

CREATING A
BULLET-PROOF IDENTITY

"The whole system of identification for people in the United States and most foreign countries is a house of cards. And it's erected on soft, dry sand." — **Gray, in a conversation with the author.**

I was in the San Francisco International Airport waiting to catch a plane to Texas when I met the man who provided most of the information for this chapter. He was a smallish man with a neatly-trimmed gray beard, wore an expensive gray suit and carried an aluminum Halliburton attache case which was quite the worse for wear and was also gray in hue. I never learned his name, but I've come to think of him as "Gray."

I struck up a conversation with him because he was such a contrast to the good ol' boy types who filled the waiting area. We chatted in the aimless way of strangers until I casually mentioned I was researching a book on deliberate disappearances and identity changes, at which point he became electrified. I've thought back on the incident many times since and I do not believe he was a disappearee, although the information he gave me about documenting an identity has checked out 100%. Most of what follows is based on my conversations with Gray, which lasted until I deplaned in El Paso.

LOCATING AN IDENTITY

The first step in creating an identity is locating a good one to use. The word "locate" is the key here. While it is possible to *fabricate* an identity from scratch, and many people have done it successfully, it is an extremely difficult way to go about solving a simple problem. And the manufactured identity almost never withstands investigation as well as a genuine identity used by an imposter.

Almost everybody is investigated at one time or another to a greater or lesser degree. It may be the personnel department where you've applied for a job, a bonding company investigating your past before they agree to guarantee your performance, or a prospective father-in-law checking up on his daughter's suitor. Although most of these investigations are not very rigorous, it is fairly easy to turn up enough information (or the lack thereof) to spot a completely fictitious identity. On the other hand, the person who adopts a genuine identity should be able to document it thoroughly enough to avoid discovery.

Assuming a Living Identity

While it is important to build your documentation on a genuine identity, it is a mistake to assume the identity of another living person. Many small time criminals have made this mistake and it has cost them a trip back to jail. They lift a guy's wallet or find some credit cards while engaged in a robbery and go on a coast-to-coast spending spree. Maybe they just use the guy's ID and don't try to spend his money. But what they seem to forget is someone out there has an interest in locating them and putting a halt to their charade: the guy whose identity they copped. And if the theft is reported the police may be looking for someone using the victim's identity.

Of course, there are imposters who have a definite need to appropriate a specific person's identity. Even then, it is very tricky to collect documentation to support the hoax. The imposter might find himself explaining to the authorities how he managed to get a duplicate drivers license after the speeding ticket he received was traced to a man who wasn't even in town that day. The imposter's request for a copy of "his" birth certificate will leave a paper trail that's easy enough to follow. And a duplicate passport, if discovered, could lead to *serious* trouble.

When the State Department realizes it has issued passports to two different people with the same exact name and vital statistics, the shit is going to hit the fan! One passport is going to be revoked, and there are lots of places in the world where being without that little blue book could literally be a fate worse than death. Of course, it would be difficult for the State Department to cause a traveler much trouble because there are no records kept of the exact whereabouts of U.S. passport holders. The real trouble would come when the imposter tried to enter the U.S. again or renew the passport.

Then there is the danger of crossing trails with the rightful holder of your assumed identity. The chances of this are not as slight as they may seem when you include all the people who know the original person well and might take more than passing notice of the "coincidence" of names. We've all heard of the "doctor" who finds himself behind bars after the "real thing" discovers the impersonation and blows the whistle. While there may be persons who have a need to appropriate the identity of a living individual, it is decidedly a mistake for a disappearee.

In the unlikely and unwise event that the identity of another living person is assumed, it should be that of someone who is totally undistinguished and unremarkable. Doctors, lawyers, or any other professional or official persons are so thoroughly documented that the likelihood of an imposter being spotted increases dramatically. It would be much better to assume the identity of an ordinary Joe Doakes who makes his living taking the hides off dead cows or repairing golf carts.

A Built-In Second Identity

Oddly enough, some people don't have to look any further than themselves to find a suitable new identity. Millions of people in the United States are "inadvertent phantoms;" that is, their current documented identity is not the one they started out in life with. This group includes foundlings who were "given" by their parents to another couple who raised the child as their bonafide offspring, adoptees who took the name of their adopting parents without voiding their original birth records, people raised under false names so their false parents could collect more welfare benefits, etc. Many children of single mothers take the name of their "father" when mom marries or remarries.

Often the first knowledge the individual in question has of his identity situation is when he applies for a passport, or to collect Social Security or something of that nature, and discovers to his horror that there is no record whatsoever of his having been born. At least not in the place or on the date or under the name he has always regarded as his own.

Each and every one of these inadvertent identity changers has a second identity readily available. It will usually be a simple matter to document the identity he has lived with all his life, and it will also be easy to document the identity under which his birth was actually registered. For the disappearee, the only disadvantage in using his original identity is that it is a rather obvious ploy if the disappearance is thoroughly investigated by people with lots of time and money at their disposal. Of course, it is very rare for such an investigation to be conducted, so this method shouldn't be overlooked.

Resurrecting the Dead

If you aren't fortunate enought to have a built-in second identity, the best way to get an identity is to use one that no one needs anymore: the identity of someone that's died. One of the beautiful things about the United States is that there's very little correlation between birth and death records. The official papers on births and deaths are kept in the smallest political subdivisions, such as towns, cities and counties. There is no central federal agency that keeps tabs on all this information. And the rules and regulations on recording births and deaths differ from state to state.

Because a great many people die without enough documentation on them to establish their place of birth, there are a huge number of identities that can be appropriated simply by finding their birth place and getting a copy of their birth certificate. Chances are that you will be able and willing to do a more thorough job of researching the deceased's identity than the bureaucrats who handled the official paperwork when he died. Let's look at some of the ways to find the right corpse.

War Buddies

A friend that you went through the service with, and that either died in combat or is "missing in action" is an excellent choice. You probably know a fair amount about his life to help you back up your new identity. Since he died outside the United States, there is a good chance his death was not officially registered in the town where he was born. This method is even better if your buddy never got around to getting a Social Security card, but there are ways to resolve that problem.

Childhood Friend

For many of the same reasons, the friend who died as a child is as good a choice as the war buddy. You may know a great deal about your childhood friend's early life that will help support your ruse. If he died in a city other than the one he was born in, chances are there are no records of his death in his hometown.

Headstones

If you can't think of someone you know personally that died in youth, you can cruise the graveyards in any town looking at the tombstones. These usually give the deceased's original name, date of birth and date of death. Sometimes they include the names of the parents and the place of death, which only make it easier to then get the ID you need.

Newspapers

A logical place to look for an identity is the obituary columns of newspapers. These are particularly good sources in small towns and rural areas because there are fewer obits to wade through, and because they usually give much more detail about the deceased's family, age, place of birth and death, and reason for death. You can then investigate anyone of the proper age who was born in a distant city.

Another item to look for is newspaper accounts of disasters like plane crashes, train derailments, volcanoes, tidal waves, fires, etc. Many times the papers will give a list of those who died in such accidents. If the death happened outside of U.S. territory then there is almost no chance that the individual's birth records have been connected with the death.

Personnel Records

If you have access to the personnel records of a large company, an employment agency or a government agency, you're In Like Flynn. In the records you'll find complete dossiers of dozens of employees, ex-employees, deceased employees, and all their families. The information will likely include background, education, and the name, place and date of birth all neatly spelled out. The names of relatives, friends, past employers and where they live may also be in the files — all grist for the mill of the identity changer. Sometimes there are separate files for deceased employees, which makes the job easier; while most companies are very protective of their personnel files, they don't worry that much about the silent majority.

The Right Fit

It is easy enough to find the identity of a dead person to acquire — someone whose birth and death records never crossed — and you can therefore be a little bit choosey about exactly which identity you take. You want an identity that suits your purposes well, so it is best to consider some of the secondary characteristics of the identity you are going to appropriate.

There are advantages and disadvantages to certain surnames. Don't choose a name like "John Smith" or "John Doe," because such a name cries out to be investigated if you ever get stopped by a police officer. The best names seem to be those from the British Isles or Northern Europe because they are fairly common all over the U.S. One name may fit great in Flint, Michigan but go over like a lead balloon in Flippin, Arkansas.

Spanish or Spanish-sounding surnames should be avoided. This is due to the immigration difficulties between the U.S. and its neighbors to the South. Anyone with a Spanish-sounding surname is checked much more thoroughly at the border with Mexico. In fact, I've seen immigration officers interrogating Hispanics in bus stations as far north as Albuquerque, New Mexico. While the name is really a small detail, it is the details that often trip up identity changers.

You also want to look at the education of the person whose identity you're taking. Hopefully, they already have a good college degree that will help you get a job. If not, you may have to go back to school, which is not as bad as it sounds. Universities are excellent places to spend time while you are getting used to your new identity. Students come under less scrutiny than your average working stiff. Also, employers and/or neighbors don't seem to ask as many questions about your past if you've only recently graduated from college.

You may want to avoid any identities that have very specialized training in their backgrounds. You would probably be foolish to acquire the ID of a doctor, not only because you will have to assemble an enormous amount of documentation to support this identity but also because you may be called on to use your professional skills — which you don't really have. Taking the identity of a demolitions expert would also be a foolish choice, because you never know when some arsonist is going to trigger a police search for people with "your" documented skills.

It would be nice if you could find the identity of someone who was engaged in work that you, yourself, can perform. Or perhaps the person whose identity you assume will have experience in an area of interest to you. If you can't find a good occupational match, the next best thing is a general kind of background that could be adapted to a variety of different jobs.

As a final note, you don't even want to think about assuming the identity of someone who left a family behind when they went. Chances are their ex-wife or kids are collecting Social Security or some other benefit as a result of the death. When you appropriate such an identity there are excellent chances that you will trigger a connection to the dead man's family. If someone's monthly check disappears because of you, it won't be long before the matter is cleared up — to your detriment.

DOCUMENTING YOUR NEW IDENTITY

As we have seen, the best way to build a new identity is to assume the identity of someone who's died without having their death officially noted in the place they were born. If you believe you have found the right identity to assume you may still have difficulty locating that person's place of birth, which is essential. Let's take a look at a few ways to uncover this information.

Several of the methods used to find a good identity will also provide the details you will need to document it. Obituaries, gravestones and newspaper accounts of disasters are all likely to contain information about the place of birth, the date of birth and the parents' names. The obituary of a person may provide the name of his former employer. Using a ruse you may be able to obtain the information you need from his employer's personnel file. If the person was a childhood friend or relative, you probably know some people to contact that would know their date and place of birth.

I know of one instance where a person knew the name and place of residence of someone who'd died that he thought would be a good identity to assume. Using a mail drop and letterhead run off in the deceased person's name, he wrote off to the U.S. Census Bureau to see if they had any information that might help him. The Census Bureau wrote back requesting $7.50. He sent them a money order through the mail drop. The information he received in return was not only enough to get the birth certificate he needed, but was in and of itself official enough to get a passport.

If you are having a difficult time of the research or live in a distant town where records aren't handy, you can pay someone to do the research for you. Law school students or moonlighting legal researchers are the best types to hire. They don't ask too many questions and they like the color of your money. Most of them are fairly sharp, and locating birth records is child's play for them.

Birth Certificates

All identification in all countries comes back to the original registration of birth. So the first thing an identity changer needs to do is acquire the birth certificate of the original holder of the identity being assumed. To do this, you will need to know where and when the person was born and, ideally, the parents' names and the mother's maiden name.

Other than the sources already mentioned, one place to get this information is from birth notices in the newspapers. You will find that many births are never announced in the papers. This is because many of us are bastards, in more ways than one, and newspaper editors are very tactful about such matters. In fact, the birth may not be announced if the parents had a big society wedding five or six months prior to the birth. In these cases hospital records and church baptismal records may come in handy.

Once you have the proper information, you need to then request a copy of the birth certificate. You needn't be worried about arousing suspicion. Lots of people do not have either their original birth certificate or a copy. They get lost, their parents never gave it to them, they get destroyed in fires or floods, etc. In fact, the lack of an original birth certificate is so common that the U.S.

Passport Office provides information on how to go about requesting a certified copy. Contact your nearest Passport Office to get this information.

There will usually be a small fee for the duplicate birth certificate. When requesting one, you should use a letterhead run off in the name of the person whose ID you are after. You should use money orders for all payments required, and conduct your communications through a mail drop. That will make it harder for anyone looking for you to trace you, should something unexpected come up.

If you counter resistance to your request, there are ways of getting around it. I know of one stuffy county clerk who would not provide a birth certificate to a friend of mine who wanted to acquire a specific identity. My friend simply found a lawyer who had just hung out his shingle in the town where the deceased was born. My friend told the attorney that he was looking for a missing heir and needed to see the potential heir's birth certificate.

The lawyer didn't even raise an eyebrow. He said that his fee would be fifty dollars, payable in advance. My friend laid out a U.S. Grant, the lawyer deposited it in his vest pocket, then told my friend to make himself comfortable in the waiting room. The attorney then headed across town to the courthouse. A half hour later my friend had not only a certified copy of the birth certificate he wanted, but copies of both the individual's parents' birth certificates, too.

Once you have the birth certificate, getting the rest of the documents you need is a piece of cake. We'll take a look at a few of the more important pieces of ID you will want to acquire.

Social Security Number

One of the trickier pieces of ID to get will be a new Social Security number. As we stated before, it is extremely inadvisable to use the number that came with your new identity because you may cause all sorts of bells and whistles to go off at the Social Security Administration. And it is even more important not to use the number you had in your former identity, again because the inconsistency between names and numbers is going to catch up with you. The SSA may not say anything as long as you keep paying into the system, but when your turn comes to be on the receiving end, look out.

The tricky part about getting a Social Security number is making up a clever ruse to satisfy a snoopy clerk who wants to know why you're applying so late in life. First of all, it's none of their business. No one says you have to tell them anything. Their job is to take names and issue numbers. And most clerks will do just that. They don't get paid a fortune to fill out those forms, so chances are they aren't too sophisticated and probably don't give a damn. But if you don't want to draw any unnecessary attention to yourself, it could be handy to have a ruse at the ready.

There are a lot of logical reasons for a person not to get a Social Security number until late in life. A person just released from an institution like a prison or a mental hospital may never have had a card. Someone who's been a "perpetual student" spending years accumulating degrees may not have one. Probably the best ruse is that you've been living abroad since your parents moved to Canada when you were a teenager. Any of these ruses should be enough to bore the clerk into issuing the number.

Drivers License

Once you have your birth certificate you can run down to the Department of Motor Vehicles and land a drivers license. The respect given to a drivers license as positive identification is astonishing, even comforting, though by no means is it justified by the evidence. The drivers license is almost universally demanded when cashing checks, which is why check artists always have a license at the ready. I've known people who offered their passports with recent photos as proof of their identification and had them turned down in favor of the drivers license. And passports contain more thorough information and are more expensive and harder to obtain than a drivers license.

There is some justification for the affinity for drivers licenses. In most states a drivers license is the only thing a person carries in the way of identification that has his photograph on it, although some states use a thumb print. Clerks in stores are trained to ask for a drivers license and *only* a drivers license when cashing checks. So few people in the U.S. have passports that offering one only confuses the help.

From a professional identification man's point of view, a thumb print is a far better method of establishing an identity than a photograph. But for the shopkeeper who doesn't have the time or technical ability to compare prints, the photograph is the best basis for swapping his merchandise for a piece of paper. In fact, the drivers license is such a popular piece of ID that many states issue non-drivers licenses. While it really isn't a "license" at all, since it doesn't permit the holder to *do* anything, it is useful and readily accepted as a form of personal identification.

As far as ruses go, there are many more reasons for not having a drivers license late in life than a social security number. Many people simply don't have the money together to buy a car until they get up in their years. Another very rational explanation is that you've been living in New York, where a person would have to be insane to drive regularly. If you really want to do it up right, you could enroll in drivers education through one of the many schools that offer this service. When you finish the course, most schools will hand you a diploma to show the DMV people. Some schools will even have someone accompany you personally through your tests, or the DMV will send out an officer to test all the graduates at the school.

Along with your birth certificate you will want to bring a couple letters addressed to you as proof of your residence. It should be easy enough to arrange for them to show your mail drop address rather than your actual residence. But if you're like most disappearees, you won't have much use for your drivers license other than as identification, at least immediately. That's because it's foolish to take your old car with you into your new identity, as previously explained. Also, traffic violations are the downfall of many an identity changer not yet comfortable in their new life and ill-prepared for the probing questions of the traffic cop.

Passports

And now for the granddaddy of all forms of personal identification: the U.S. passport. Impressive as this document may sound, it is relatively easy to get as long as you have the proper back-up ID, and as long as you know a bit about the procedure involved before you start out.

Passports are issued primarily by the U.S. Passport Office division of the State Department. There are U.S. Passport Offices in most major cities. If there is no passport office in your area, they may be issued by the Clerk of the Federal Court. In some instances they are even handled by local U.S. Post Offices.

For the identity switcher, far and away the best place to go is the Passport Office. The Clerk of the Court and especially the Post Office people are not likely to have much experience with passports and they will want all the "i"s dotted and "t"s crossed, twice. At the Passport Office your application will be handled by a bunch of bored civil servants who are so used to the routine that they won't remember you seven seconds after you walk out the door.

The Passport Clerk will ask you for your birth certificate and some form of supporting photo ID, like your drivers license. They will then give you a form to fill out and return with a couple of passport photos and the fee, currently $35. Passport photos are fairly special, and must be taken according to specific regulations which change from time to time. It's best to use one of the passport photo places that are often located right near the passport office. They know the requirements and they generally can have your pictures ready while you wait. It's best to get several sets of extra copies if you plan to travel outside the U.S. much. Many countries require the same kind of photos for travel documents they issue to foreigners, and you don't want to have to find some advanced country where you can get your pictures taken properly before resuming your travels.

The best time of year to get your passport is during the winter months, if you want to have it mailed to you in a reasonable period of time. Thousands of tourists trot down to the local Passport Office about two weeks before their 21-country summer cruise is due to depart. Even if they planned well in advance to take their trip, they forget about the passport until the last minute. It can take several months for your passport to arrive if you apply at the peak travel times.

A passport is now good for ten years. When you turn in your application, photos and fee, you should ask for the larger, 48-page booklet. The standard 24-page passport gets filled up quickly if you travel extensively outside the United States. When your passport expires, renewing it is easy. You simply go to the Passport Office with your old passport, a new set of pictures and the fee, and you're on your way again.

There is one odd facet to the passport application process. For some reason, the clerks always ask you for the exact countries you intend to visit. This makes absolutely no sense at all, since once the passport is issued you are free to go anywhere you like, and this regardless of the crap printed in the front of the document about not being able to go to Cuba, North Korea, etc. It really doesn't matter what you tell them, just so long as you don't say you're on a business trip to Libya or some other place currently on the federal government's shit-list.

Fake ID

For those disappearees attempting to create a new identity totally from scratch, fake ID will provide an important part of their documentation needs. There are many companies that will sell you an official looking birth certificate in any name you need. These mail order certificates are authentic looking enough to use in getting a legitimate drivers license (but *not* a passport!). In fact, if you are having trouble obtaining the data you need to get a copy of a real birth certificate, you might consider getting a fake one, using it to obtain other legitimate ID, and then destroying the birth certificate to keep your trail clean.

You can also get fake drivers licenses and identity cards, but the better route is to use a fake birth certificate to get legitimate photo ID. Why settle for second best?

While fake ID is not a good substitute for legitimate documentation like drivers licenses and passports, it is extremely helpful to the identity changer in providing supporting ID and fleshing out the new identity. There is a good publication on this subject listed in the reference chapter. It describes how to get and use fake ID, lists the companies that sell it, shows pictures of the items for sale, and gives prices where available.

You can buy all sorts of ID to fill out the identity you've chosen. If you are looking to a professional work life you can buy all kinds of diplomas, certificates showing membership in professional organizations, certificates of merit and commendation, even college transcripts. At the other end of the scale, you can buy fake union membership cards, journeymen's cards and certificates that indicate completion of a variety of technical training courses. If you'd like a family, you can buy marriage certificates, school records for your fictitious children, even divorce papers. While this ID will not withstand the simplest of investigations, it is the kind of stuff that will rarely be looked at closely and where detection of your fraud probably won't get you into a lot of trouble. And it certainly adds meat to a well-thought-out identity.

Forged ID

For those having difficulty getting legitimate pieces of fake ID and considering purchasing forged ID on the street, my advice is DON'T. When you buy ID off the street, you don't know what you're getting into. First, forged documents are often exorbitantly expensive. The people you are buying them from have good reason to believe you are in desperate need of them, or else why go to such lengths to get them? They will charge you accordingly. If you are trying to get a forged passport so you can leave the country in a hurry, you should realize that it will often take as long to find a good forgery as it will to get the real thing issued under an assumed identity.

Second, when you buy forged documents off the street, you leave yourself at the mercy of the parties who sold them to you. The degree of cooperation between the police and small-time crooks in this country is amazing. They work on a *quid-pro-quo* basis whereby the police won't disrupt the illegal operation as long as they get either a cut or a little information now and then. And in no case does this system work better than with purveyors of forged documents. While their trade is illegal, the information they can provide is worth far more to the police than it is to crack down on them. The document forger earns twice off the naive purchaser: first by the outrageous price he charges you for the goods, and second by giving your name to the cops to "pay his rent."

The third reason to stay away from forged documents is that, rather than being forged, the documents are more than likely stolen. If you go running around with someone else's drivers license or passport, you are just begging for trouble. Chances are the original theft was reported to the authorities. They will be looking for someone using that name and trying to cash checks or make purchases using the stolen ID. And if you try to leave the country with a stolen passport that was probably reported missing before you even bought it, good luck. Stolen and forged ID is responsible for bringing down a lot of fugitives from the law who didn't have the time, foresight or resources to document a legitimate alternative identity. In short, if you don't need forged ID, don't get it. And if for some reason it's the only way to go, then get rid of it as fast as you can and pick up a legitimate identity.

COPING

"In a money society you can be independent with money, or independent without money. Anywhere in between you're under the thumb." —**Michael Collins in *The Brass Rainbow*.**

You have seen that documenting a new identity is not all that difficult. In fact, the hardest aspect of disappearing and switching identities is coping with the change in lifestyle as you establish yourself as a new person. The story of the prison escapee who has led a happy and sedate life as an auto mechanic for years only to be tripped-up by some trivial happenstance is a staple item in the newspapers. Even clever and well-planned disappearances like that of Larry Lavin's as told previously can be unravelled through a couple of seemingly insignificant oversights. The successful disappearee, especially one who is earnestly sought, must be able to land on his feet like the proverbial cat and move quickly and carefully thereafter.

The problems of the disappearee become critical the minute he walks out on his original identity and into a new one, regardless of whether the new identity has been groomed well in advance. He is immediately confronted with the questions of where to go, how to get work, and whether or not he should disguise himself. All the aspects of every day life we all take for granted are enormous problems for the newly-disappeared that must be solved promptly and correctly. One mistake along the way could take months of work to correct, perhaps forcing a second switch in identity, or perhaps leading to his discovery.

WHERE TO GO

The most immediate and pressing issue the disappearee must handle is where to go. The first few days of a disappearance are a sensitive time, for this is when the loudest cry will be raised over your vanishing act and when the pursuit will be most intense. It is also likely that you will still be in the near vicinity for awhile, making detection from a wide variety of sources possible. The vanisher must find a safe haven where he can think through his next moves and marshall his resources for the long road ahead.

One of the more elaborate transitions from old life to new I heard was related to me in a bar in Oakland, California. I was involved in a general discussion of disappearances and identity changing with a slim, tanned, well-spoken individual of about fifty years of age. When I mentioned that the first part of an identity change is the hardest, but that thorough planning could smooth out most of the rough spots, he smiled widely and nodded his agreement.

"A few years back I had a friend who vanished," he began. "He was living — existing really — in, well, one of those jerkwater towns in the flat country where you can see the great distances without seeing anything at all. He was a fishing nut and was terribly disappointed that the environs he lived in had no outlet for his favorite pursuit. Sure, there were muddy little creeks near his home filled with bullhead and carp and catfish, but he was a dry-fly purist, and you know how a died-in-the-wool, tie-your-own-flies fisherman feels about such trash."

I nodded my sympathy.

He continued, "The trouble was, his wife didn't like the amount of time and money he spent going to places where the fish live. He was a respectable financial executive, and she was a sucker for lost causes. Ever since their kids had gone through college and moved away, she got more and more involved in volunteer work. That would have been fine with him, except that she was using his position to advance her causes, and she expected — no, demanded — that he attend all kinds of fundraising events and be photographed with disabled kids and the like. It was more than he could stomach.

"I don't know exactly when or how he hit upon the idea of chucking it all and starting a new life under a different name. The idea just seemed to grow. Once he accepted it, he began to make his plans. One of the first things he did was buy a pick-up truck with an insulated, all-weather camper already installed. He purchased it in a distant city that he visited regularly on business. And he paid for it with an unexpected company bonus he received."

"Didn't his wife know anything about their finances?" I asked. "Seems she would have known about the bonus because of the income tax angle."

"No, she didn't know anything about it. It was one of those end-of-the-year deals, and he received the money in February. That gave him about fourteen months before it would show up on the IRS forms, which was plenty of time for him to execute his plan."

"Anyway, he bought the camper under his new name. The dealer was very helpful arranging the insurance and licensing. He stored the camper with the dealer, picking it up occasionally for short trips when he could sneak the time."

"Where did he get the new identity?" I asked. "Just make it up out of whole cloth?"

He gave me a sly look. "No, he'd started reading up on the subject and then he remembered that he had an older brother who died when he was less than a year old. My parents never mention him, and I had no reason to ever tell my wife about my brother. Christ, I wasn't even born when he died!"

He abruptly stopped at this point, realizing he'd slipped out of the third person. He considered whether to continue or not. At last he went on.

"There was a lot of local interest in my friend's disappearance, but as far as I know, no one ever made the connection between him and his brother. It was a perfect identity to slip into because he didn't have to memorize a lot of strange data about place of birth, mother's maiden name, and so on."

"Where did he go when he walked out?" I asked.

"Well the first thing he did was make a fishing trip to end all fishing trips. He lashed flies across every trout stream of note between Kuskokwim in Western Alaska and the little streams on the western slopes of the Sierra Madre Occidentales in Mexico."

"What did he do for money?" I wondered.

"He had a small amount of savings with him when he left. You'd be surprised how little it costs for a man to live in a camper by himself. But without any credit available to him, it wasn't long before he had to seek out work. Even though he was a paper-shuffler in his former life, he had a lot of practical carpentry skills he'd learned fixing up the houses he'd lived in. So he earned money as he went along doing odd jobs and the like, though he was in no condition for heavy physical labor.

"After a while he assembled a decent set of tools and a few good contacts along his favorite routes. He was then able to work a few days a week and spend the rest of his time traveling and fishing. He's since joined a carpenters union and works out of the hall whenever the mood or the need strikes him."

"Sounds kinda romantic to me," I said. "Traveling the country carefree without a responsibility in the world. I imagine it gets a bit lonely, though."

"I suppose it could," he said, "but it doesn't have to be. There are a lot of people out there doing exactly the same thing. You quickly develop a comradery with these other nomads, and nobody ever asks you much about your past or your personal life. My friend eventually latched onto a woman who is a full professor at a university. She's not interested in marriage and she sure can handle a fly rod. They spend a lot of time together in the summers, though he doesn't hang around when school's in session."

Perhaps he felt he talked a little too much and with a bit more enthusiasm than he'd intended, for he abruptly changed the subject. We chatted away about nothing in particular until he finished his beer, whereupon he headed for the door. After he was gone I asked the barkeep if he knew the fellow I was talking with.

"No," he said. "He's not a regular — just comes in once a month or so for lunch and a beer. He's not much of a talker. In fact, I think him talking to you was his first real conversation in this place. He really loves to fish, though. A friend of mine told me he was working on a building job here a while back, earning pretty good money as a carpenter, when he pulled the pin to go off trout fishing before the job was done. Can you beat that?"

Transportation

The unique aspect of the above disappearance is the transportation used. The disappearee prepared his transportation in advance. Most disappearees will not have the money to buy a car before they go. And as I have said previously, it is very unwise to take your old car with you into your new life.

If you do use a car to effect your disappearance, there are a number of ways to get rid of it. If you simply refuse to part with it then you should make plans in advance to store it for a while until whoever may be looking for you gets tired of the chase. The best bet for storage is to rent a lock-up garage in a residential neighborhood. This way the car will remain out of sight and you aren't likely to face a lot of prying questions as long as the rent is paid. When things cool down a little you may be able to find a buyer for the car who won't be too concerned about the legal formalities of the deal. You shouldn't even consider taking the car out of storage and using it again, unless you don't value your new identity very much.

Another way to get rid of your car once you have found your destination is to have it stolen. Simply drive your car into one of the poorer looking neighborhoods of a big city, park it on a residential street and leave the keys in the car and the doors unlocked. Before morning your car will probably have changed hands several times. Within a few days it should have a new paint job and a fresh set of plates.

One disappearee I talked with escaped by driving his car to the airport where he parked it, hopped an airport bus to the Greyhound station and there boarded another bus to his destination. All he took with him was a suitcase. Judging from the efforts made to find him, I imagine his "luggage" consisted of a considerable amount of someone else's money. The police discovered his car at the airport and spent several days circulating pictures of him to ticket agents, hostesses, etc. I found this to be a very clever way to throw people off the trail.

If you expect to be the object of a vigorous search, then bus transportation is an excellent way to go. Bus lines do not keep passenger lists. Nor do they require that you show ID to get a ticket. And fellow passengers on buses seem to be less concerned about who they're traveling with than your typical airline passenger.

But don't let the passenger lists scare you off from using a commercial airline. Ticket agents don't care what a passenger calls himself, as long as he pays the fare up front. In fact, every time a large, commercial flight crashes there are unidentified passengers. The people holding the names on the passenger list are often alive and well and may never have set foot on a plane in their life. You will have to wait until your new identity is documented before you board an international flight — passengers headed overseas are required to show their passport prior to boarding.

Renting a car is probably not an option for most vanishers. First, it's expensive. Most people who disappear are short enough on money without blowing half of it on a car rental. But more importantly, you'd be hard pressed to rent a car anywhere in America without a credit card. It doesn't matter how much money you wave in their faces; rental car companies won't even look at you if you can't come across with a VISA or American Express. And if there's one thing a recent disappearee lacks, it's credit.

The First Days

Unless you've prepared your disappearance well in advance or have a lot of money, you may have trouble finding a place to sleep until you get on your feet. A surprising number of disappearees stay with friends or relatives the first couple of nights. This is usually a mistake. These are the first places someone will come looking for you. Also, you leave a trail that could be easy to trace. A great deal of pressure may come to bear on your friends or relatives once you're gone if the people looking for you have good reason to suspect they gave you safe harbor.

One interesting exception to this rule was a disappearee I talked to who moved in with a former girlfriend. He claims he picked his destination city more or less at random. Once there he discovered that his old flame lived in that town. After a couple days of putting up in boxcars for the night he decided to give her a call. She invited him for dinner, which turned out to be one of those sentimental red-wine-and-candles affairs. Love was kindled anew, the upshot being he moved in for an extended stay.

"What story did you tell her to account for your new identity?" I asked him.

"Oh, I told her that I went through bankruptcy and my attorney told me I would never be able to get credit or do business under my own name again, so I adopted a new one. It was pretty thin, but people believe what they *want* to believe, and she wanted to believe that *every* word I told her was the truth."

"So what happened after you left her place?" I asked.

He chortled loud, clear and joyous. "Hell, I never did leave! We've got two kids in school and now both of us have damn good jobs. No sense in splitting on a problem-free situation, is there?"

Taking up with a member of the opposite sex is actually a pretty good idea for the newly disappeared. Of course, shacking up with an old girlfriend is not a good idea for most people, because they will know about both of your identities and if things don't work out as well as they did for the fellow above, your spurned love may go running to the people you are trying to get away from.

A stranger in a bar who doesn't know anything about your past — only your present — is another thing altogether. They may provide you with food, shelter and a mailing address while you're getting your new identity established. And if things turn sour and you haven't told all about your former life, you won't have to fear any anonymous letters to your ex-wife, or whoever.

Shacking up with someone sure beats sleeping on a park bench. As I noted in an earlier chapter, living off the street is not a very good idea for the newly disappeared. You are likely to be surrounded by an assortment of petty crooks and drifters. This crowd is carefuly watched by the police, lest they start to infect the decent folk of the town who pay the taxes that pay their salaries.

If you're really down on your money, a mission is a much better place to stay than on the streets. Contrary to popular opinion, they aren't just for drunks and bums. Many a vanisher has spent his first few nights as the guest of the Salvation Army. They've assisted many, many people who are looking to make a new start in life, and they aren't inclined to make embarrassing inquiries.

When all is said and done, there is no substitute for money when undertaking an identity change. I know of one disappearee who went so far as to take out a second mortgage on his home to finance his leave. There are many places one can go with money, and cash seems to answer all those prying questions with more authority than half-a-dozen credit cards or other pieces of ID. Many people have enough money to travel when they disappear. In fact, the desire to travel is one of the main motivations to disappear (when combined with family and other problems). And travel is an excellent choice, for it allows the disappearee the time and peace of mind to consider his possibilities and chart a new course.

Finding a Place to Live

Some disappearees are able to live like turtles, carrying their lives with them in their campers like the fly-fishing gentleman we met earlier. But if you aren't planning to live on the move like a nomad, going into the back country can be a dangerous proposition.

Small-town U.S.A. is bad news for a recent disappearee. The locals in small communities have an overwhelming interest in "outsiders" and derive their principal entertainment from speculating endlessly about everyone in sight. A stranger is something to notice in such towns. Anything foreign about you will immediately be held up to public scrutiny. This is hardly a desireable environment for a person with a young identity to age.

A fresh disappearee should probably look for a more permissive town. By that, I mean a city where the authorities are not preoccupied with enforcing a host of ridiculous nuisance laws. San Francisco and the surrounding Bay Area seem to be very attractive to identity changers for precisely this reason. Not only are people less inclined to pry into your private life in such places, but it can be very enjoyable to live in a city where "anything goes."

A large city is better than a small one for a number of other reasons. A stranger won't stand out much in a city of millions. Public transportation is usually well established in large cities, which is helpful to those who have disappeared without a lot of money. There are more job opportunities of a greater variety in a large city. And there are also more resources of the type an identity changer is likely to need: mail drops, secretarial services, community colleges, etc.

Many disappearees make a checklist of the things they regard as necessary when picking a town in which to begin a new life, and this strikes me as a good idea. It would obviously be stupid for a literate man, a man who enjoys intelligent conversation and is used to elaborate library facilities, to attempt to exist in Mott, North Dakota or Mount Shasta City, California. Similarly, an individual really hooked on huntin' and fishin' and the outdoor life would be a fool to head for Washington, D.C.

Here's an interesting note about the residences that some disappearees choose. Several of my contacts specifically mentioned that they always wanted a second exit in any place they lived. One such person kept a climbing rope in his bedroom with one end tied to the bedstead. He explained this arrangement to his nosy apartment manager by telling her that he was pathologically afraid of fire because his home had burned down when he was a small child.

FINDING WORK

With five notable exceptions, nearly everyone in our society works at a job of some kind and is automatically suspected of all kinds of dark and nefarious deeds if he doesn't work. The exempt classifications: The very rich, who obviously don't need to bother working, the very poor, who also don't need to work because the Welfare State takes care of them. Then housewives, students and retirees. Everyone else in the U.S. and Canada is expected to work or at least have the appearance of working.

I say "the appearance of working" because even if a lamster doesn't need to work for wages he should cultivate regular workman-like habits. He should leave his lodgings at the same time every day, whether he spends his time at the library or at the beach, and return home at the same time each evening. The disappearee should attempt to structure his life so as to call as little attention to himself as possible. There are just too many people who make it their business to know other people's business, especially the female who is shut up in her house all day in a residential neighborhood with too much time on her hands and too little to occupy her mind.

Most disappearees will not have the option of staying unemployed, at least not for long. When their savings run out, which could be as soon as fifteen minutes after they walk into their new life, they'll need to get a job. Trying to collect welfare on a freshly manufactured identity is a big mistake because of all the government paperwork involved and the scrutiny of public servants that results. For the typical disappearee, the question is not whether to work, but what work to do and how to get it.

There are many good reasons for working besides the need for income. One is the need to establish credit. The ability to use credit is almost a requirement for membership in our society, and people who grant credit are more impressed with a job than anything else — a steady job, that is. Any job. For oddly enough, people who grant credit are much more favorably inclined toward a laborer who makes $10,000 a year than to a writer, artist or door-to-door salesman who makes four or five times that. The writer, artist, etc. doesn't fit their pattern, and doesn't march to the sound of a time clock.

Another reason for working is that it is about the best place to make personal contacts. Loneliness is a severe problem for many identity changers, and not a small number of them have crawled back to their old lives for precisely this reason. But most jobs bring with them all sorts of social activities, and a lamster who takes part in these will have no more problems with loneliness.

Choosing an Occupation

Choosing an occupation can be a difficult process for some disappearees. If you do not have your new identity well-established in advance, you may have difficulty finding exactly the kind of work you like to do. Employers will be reluctant to hire you for a high paying job if you can't provide them with any previous work references or show training or schooling. Your first few jobs may be low-paying, part-time work where few questions are asked. After a time you can build up an employment history and a number of references that will lead you to greener pastures.

The problems of the well-to-do disappearee are often much more severe than those of the common laborer who leaves his wife. The higher a person's socio-economic status, theoretically the harder it will be to regain an equivalent position in the new identity. And the problems in finding new work are compounded by the fact that the people these disappearees leave behind often have more resources and more incentive to track them down. Further, it takes more in the way of paper qualifications to land a high-paying, high-status job than it does to pick apples.

But the well-to-do disappearee can work himself up into a nice position if he has some valuable skills to sell. Like the less-well-off laborer, he can freelance his services, say preparing taxes during tax season or doing freelance computer work, until he builds up enough references to land a decent full-time job. He should avoid jobs that are very similar to his previous employment, though. For while the United States is large geographically, it is small insofar as specialized occupations and interests are concerned. A top banker from New York City who wanders into a bank in Seattle has a good chance of meeting someone he saw at a convention.

Most people who switch identities automatically change occupations, too. In many cases the dissatisfaction with the daily grind is what causes people to disappear in the first place. Most white collar workers who disappear actually seek out blue collar work as the preferred way to earn their living. But blue collar workers seldom seek out white collar work. Rather, they change to a different but similar trade than they previously practiced.

There are a great many jobs that pay rather well for only part-time or irregular work. The construction industry is a good example, where employment tends to run along boom and bust lines. At times when the local construction unions cannot fill all the orders for manpower, there is an excellent chance of getting work even for those without developed skills. And for those who have a background as carpenters or electricians, there is always piecemeal work available, even if it's just filling in for people who are sick or on vacation.

Where construction work pays the best, which is usually in the big cities that disappearees like because it's easier to stay lost in them, unions dominate the work and effectively exclude outsiders. There are ways to work into the unions, though. One is to get a union job in areas of the country where they are less well developed, then take your membership with you to the big city once you're established. Or you can hang out at the union halls long enough to get a fill-in job, which can easily qualify you for union membership if you work it long enough.

One of the nicer aspects of landing union membership in the construction trade is that you can work out of hiring halls. These are usually operated jointly by employers and the unions. In essence, they are extremely efficient, low-fee employment agencies. Through the halls you can get short term work all over the country. And if you are in a mind to stay put for a while, you can earn excellent money. I know of people who earn upwards of $40,000 per year working out of hiring halls — plus some fantastic tax-free benefits.

There are a lot of other jobs where references and an employment track record are not required. During the good weather months nearly anyone of able body can find some sort of home improvement work to do. There is also a great deal of work available through temporary employment agencies, particularly office work. Temporary agencies usually ask a lot less questions about your background than full-blown employment agencies which disappearees should definitely avoid. The other nice facet of temporary work is that it very often leads to a full-time position with whatever company you start out with.

There is one kind of work that the vanisher should by all means avoid, and that is positions that put him in the public eye. Fields like television, radio, bartending, lecturing, bellhopping, etc., should be consistently avoided. I once knew of an accountant from Ketchikan, Alaska who had trouble keeping his clients' money separate from his own. He skipped bail and moved to Portland where he got a job hopping bells in a hotel. About a half-hour after the first Alaskan checked in, he was on an escorted, expense-paid trip back to the Land of the Midnight Sun. As obvious as this point may seem, publicity of this sort (that is, of the kind that could easily have been avoided) has been the downfall of a considerable number of lamsters and fugitives.

Landing the Job

If you're not big on part-time manual labor and desire more permanent work that you can't land with a big smile and a "how do you do," you'll need some references. If paper is what it takes to get that job, then by all means, give them the paper they want.

A couple of mail drops will come in handy at this stage of identity building. You can use them as addresses of fictitious companies that you've worked for. The names of the companies should be vague-sounding so you can claim a variety of different types of responsibilities depending on the job you're applying for. Then you get letterheads printed for these companies and write your own letters of reference or respond to your potential employers' requests for information.

You shouldn't need more than two job references to land another job. This shows your stability as an employee, and more than two is difficult to manage in that you'll need a mail drop for each reference. Besides, the signatures at the bottom of those glowing recommendations may start to look a bit similar to your prospective employer. If someone asks you for phone references, you can simply tell them that your immediate manager retired or went to work for a competitor. You may be able to swing one phone reference through a friend posing as a former employer or through a secretarial service that always tells callers the person they want is in a meeting.

The single most important thing to remember when doing battle with personnel departments is to never give a background too far different from the one required for the job you're applying for. If you're looking for a job on an assembly line somewhere it does absolutely no good to brag about your Ph.D. in English Literature. Personnel people try to never hire a skilled or highly skilled person for an unskilled job. They are fully aware that when a better job opens down the line, the over-skilled employee will be off like a shot out of a cannon.

Resist the temptation to assume any special honors that happen to come with your new identity. The reason for this is simple. A lot of these honors are bestowed on only a very few members of the profession or trade recognizing the honor. The honors are usually well-publicized and, if it's an honor worth using, it's probably sought after by many people in the field.

For example, if you assume the identity of an amateur photographer who was a Fellow of the Photographic Society of America, it would be foolish to use the designation FPSA in connection with any photographic endeavor. The minute a picture appears in a publication credited to "Lawrence Miller, FPSA" it will immediately receive close examination from all the other FPSA's and the guardians of the Society's good name. As soon as they figure out that Lawrence Miller did not take that picture (perhaps Lawrence was a sports photographer and your picture appears in *National Geographic)* the cry of fraud will be raised. This is the last thing the lamster needs!

Although when one assumes another person's identity he will almost automatically assume his education, it is not wise to attempt to "use" his degrees. Higher degrees bring

84

with them a whole package of "fellowship." This includes alumni of the colleges he attended. If you happen to cross paths with a "fellow alumnus," he will want to chat at great length about all the little pleasures of life at a school you never attended. And if you are a great distance from your alma-mater, even people who are only familiar with the school but never attended it will want to discuss geography with you.

The more prestigious and rare your degree, the greater the risk you run in using it. MD's are documented up one side and down the other and are monitored by professional associations and state agencies. Your "fellow MD's" won't take long to see through your scheme, if for no other reason than to limit their competition. And if you claim a Harvard education, you are going to attract a lot more interest than if you completed your schooling at a community college in Toledo.

If you feel you must have educational credentials it is much better to buy degrees mail order than to use the ones that came with your new shell. At least you won't have to worry about running into fellow alumnus — and if you do, they won't be in any position to blow the whistle on you.

Still another route is to go through the educational process and get a new set of your own degrees. If you've already been that route, you can shave a few years off your studies by taking waiver exams. Many disappearees want to change the direction of their lives anyway, so there is a double reason to go back to school. And a university is perhaps the best place in the world to lay low while establishing your new identity. The social climate is generally free and easy, jobs without strings attached are readily available, and the world in general doesn't make the kind of demanding requirements on college students that it expects of the average working stiff.

Many disappearees I talked to were apprehensive about not being able to take their military records into their new lives with them. They had served honorably in one branch or another of the Armed Forces. While they were in the service they were told how valuable their military experience would be in finding a job. And they were of course told that no reputable employer would allow someone with less than an honorable discharge onto the premises.

Most of them realized, though, that no employer had ever asked to see their discharge papers. They also knew that many of their contemporaries who avoided military service seemed to get along just fine. Even out-and-out draft evasion didn't seem to damage one's ability to make a living.

If by chance you assumed the identity of an old war buddy, though, don't think of assuming his rank and background, and especially not his veterans benefits. This would be out and out fraud and highly illegal. Besides, the Veterans Administration has records coming out the wazoo and chances are you wouldn't get away with the deception for very long.

HOW TO GET CREDIT

Establishing credit is important to most disappearees, as it is for the rest of the population. At first blush it would appear that getting credit could pose quite a problem for the vanisher. And it is true that the person who takes a new identity will not be able to get immediate credit. While it will take time to build up a credit rating, it is not at all difficult.

The credit people look for two things before allowing credit: a steady job and evidence of having paid bills promptly in the past. Most disappearees need to find work immediately in order to survive. That takes care of the first requirement. Again, it is better if the job is regular and

86

steady. Credit departments look askance at the writer or the door-to-door salesman, regardless of their income.

As to the second requirement, the heart of the problem is getting that first credit purchase. From then on, it's all downhill.

In any town of any size there are "jewelry stores" with their display windows filled with schlock and a snake-like character lurking in the doorway waiting to pounce on prospective customers. These places operate on the very small down payment plan. They figure that if they can get five dollars down on a $25 watch that they only paid five dollars for in the first place, any future payments are just so much gravy. They judge your credit worthiness by the clothes you wear and how clean you are, and even then their standards aren't very high. If you look decent and *tell them* you have a steady job, they will let you walk out with anything under a couple hundred bucks for a ten percent down payment. They know that a few people are going to rip them off, but on the other hand enough people will end up paying ten times what an item is worth on the "easy payment plan" to make it a very profitable business.

Buy a cheap bauble in one of these places, on the installment plan of course. Then make all the payments regularly. After you have the merchandise paid off you can move up to the kind of place that doesn't drag customers off the street by brute force. Small artsy-craftsy stores are an excellent choice. Again, the mark-up is high, even though the crafts people that make the stuff barely eek out a living. Many artists are willing to sell their work on the installment plan because it is important for them to move merchandise if they are ever going to get a good reputation.

With these two references you should be able to get a credit card from a local department store, like Macy's. With your job and your credit references they will be willing to extend you a nominal line of credit, usually about $300 to start. A couple of these cards, if worked properly, could lead you all the way to the big time: bank credit and major credit cards such as VISA or MasterCard. On the other hand, if you aren't careful to pay down your balances, they could lead you into serious debt problems, which may have been your reason for disappearing in the first place!

Don't worry if you aren't immediately accepted by the big credit card companies. Your recently cultivated credit record built up through nickle-and-dime retailers will be good enough to get you a car on the deferred payment plan. Being able to buy a car is the prime purpose for getting credit in the first place, because in this country having a car is almost a necessity. A car is probably the only really expensive item a single person needs. He can pay cash for room, board and clothing out of his regular income, but it is usually out of the question for him to buy an automobile this way.

If a lamster winds up doing the eight-to-five for a company that has a credit union, he should by all means join and make regular deposits. Credit unions often have plans whereby their depositors are allowed to borrow their own money for a slight charge. That is, if one has $1000 on deposit, it is dead simple to borrow $500 and pay interest on it, paying off the "loan" directly out of your paycheck. Meanwhile, your deposit pays interest to you, although at a somewhat lower rate than you are paying to the credit union. People do this all the time, for the same reason a disappearee would want to: borrowing your own money and paying it back will lead to a better credit rating than you could achieve through a dozen schlock shops.

There is one kind of credit problem that is peculiar to the identity changer. You may have assumed the identity of someone who was deep in debt himself. If the name of the person whose identity you copped is unusual, you could already be on a credit bureau's shit list without even knowing it. This is one of the reasons why an identity changer assumes only so much of another's identity as is absolutely necessary, and why it is so important to start with a new and pristine Social Security number. Most credit records these days are tied wholly or in part to the Social Security number. All it takes is the difference of one digit to completely confuse most information retrieval systems.

If the identity you assumed comes with credit problems, and your name is already on a bad-risk list, you can correct the "mistaken" identity if you have carefully documented yourself with unique ID.

DISGUISE

While a thorough search for a missing person is rarely ever conducted, a wee bit of disguise is definitely a good idea for an identity changer. The observation that "it's a small world" can be a scary but true prospect for the disappearee. Leaving his wife behind in Wilmington, Connecticut, he forgets that her sister, who he met once or twice over the holidays, lives in Carson City, Nevada — his new home. As he reaches for a piece of lingerie to purchase for his girlfriend's birthday, he turns around and who do you think is looking him over trying to think where she's seen this man before? *Gotcha!*

It never ceases to amaze me just how often I run into people I knew when I was a kid but haven't seen for years, or relatives I forgot I had, or old flames, etc. When you add to that the people you've met in your work life, friends of your friends that you've seen casually many times, and gas station attendants, barbers, grocery clerks, postal delivery people, etc., the number of people out there that are familiar enough with your face to remember who you are is staggering! All it takes is just one of them to make you and connect it with something they read about your having committed suicide, and you're a goner. Considering the possibilities, and the repercussions of being identified, a little disguise might just be the best buy in the history of insurance.

By "disguise" I do not mean the Lon Chaney, Hunchback of Notre Dame type of getup. A lamster doesn't need much of a change in appearance to effect his purposes. Even so simple an exercise as a change in clothing from what one ordinarily wears and a change in hairstyle are enough to throw off even one's friends and relatives. A detective for the California Police Department once told me that it is not at all unusual for parents searching Berkeley's Telegraph Avenue area to fail to recognize their own children when they meet them face-to-face.

There are six general ways that a person is recognized:

1) Gait.

2) Overall appearance.

3) Shape of the head and face.

4) Voice.

5) Features. Not the same as #3, above.

6) Location.

A simple disguise that changes any or all of these items of identification is all that is required for good, basic camouflage. Let's take them in order.

It is relatively easy to deliberately change the way you walk. But it is only too easy to forget to keep in character when tired, or when you think no one is watching. To rule against this contingency you can make it impossible to return to your original gait in moments of stress or absentmindedness. One way to do this is to wear shoes of different heights. A good orthopedic shoemaker could add 1/4" to the heal of one shoe and subtract the same amount from the other. You will automatically be forced to adjust your gait to compensate for the 1/2" difference.

Once you fall into your new gait it will never be forgotten as long as the trick shoes are worn, and perhaps even with regular shoes.

Another way to change your walk is to permanently attach some object inside one shoe of every pair you own or buy. As we all know too well, the smallest little particle stuck in your shoe causes enough discomfort to change the way you walk. The item should be identical for each pair of shoes, and it should be placed in exactly the same place. A good choice is a thumbtack with the pointed edge pushed into the sole of the shoe. The rounded back of the tack should be enough to alter your gait without crippling you for life.

Overall appearance is determined to a marked degree by clothing, weight and posture. Most of us have had the experience of meeting our dentist or corner policeman out of uniform and completely and embarrassingly failing to recognize him. Similarly, a man who always wears neat, conservative suits will pass unnoticed by his co-workers and associates if he meets them head-on while dressed in laborer's clothing.

It is more important, however, for a disappearee to dress so as not to attract attention than it is for him to dress for disguise. A person who was a carpenter in his old identity and switches to masonry work should not go around dressed in three-piece suits in his off hours to disguise himself. Rather, he should attempt to blend in with his surroundings as best as possible. There are other ways to alter the appearance without changing the way one dresses.

One of the surest ways to avoid recognition is to wear glasses, especially sunglasses, if you did not wear them previously. Many people look very similar if one judges them by height, weight and hair coloring. So many times someone will only recognize you at the moment they make eye contact. Clear eyeglasses are an excellent disguise for the person that never wore glasses. And while sunglasses may seem inappropriate for many occasions, a person who always wears tinted glasses or sunglasses will not stand out once people are used to them.

Some other simple methods for disguising the appearance are changing hair color and hair style, removing any jewelry that you customarily wear, wearing different colored clothing than you might normally wear, growing or shaving facial hair, and getting dentures if you've needed them for a while anyway.

A drastic weight change affects the appearance in several ways. A man who was a consistent forty pounds or more overweight in his original existence will drastically change his gait, general appearance, features and the very shape of his face simply by knocking off the spare tire. And it isn't that hard to do — I've done it myself. Several times.

The congenitally skinny people have a different weight problem, for which I know of no solution. I know several thin people who could eat everything on the menu of an Italian restaurant three times a day and not gain anything but heartburn for their efforts. These kind of people will have to find some other way to disguise themselves.

One is also recognized by the general appearance of the head and face, which is different than being recognized by your features. It is this facet of identification that enables one to recognize a friend seen dimly through the side window of his car as he drives by in the rain.

Changing the length of hair is a good way to alter the shape of the head. Your disappearance may be the occasion for a crew cut or even a Yul Brynner cue-ball bob. Eyeglasses change the shape of the head while they hide the eyes. Beards and mustaches change the shape of the face, though they may not be appropriate in certain communities or professions. Taking up smoking cigarettes or a pipe will have the effect of changing your facial appearance, particularly in profile.

It is probably more difficult to permanently change your voice than any other aspect of your identity. A person's friends can usually recognize him by voice alone. If one speaks with an accent or in a dialect it is best to get rid of it pronto and learn "standard" American English. Of course, this is easier said than done. But if a man is clever enough and determined enough to change his identity, the task of changing his language should not be beyond his reach.

A great many of our language habits are a product of the environment we find ourselves in. It is very important that the identity changer adjust his speech to fit in with his surroundings. A white collar executive who turns to the building trades in his new life better learn to cuss a good streak, and learn it quickly. Four-syllable words are seldom uttered on Alaskan fishing vessels. Highbrow language will make you stand out like a sore thumb in a blue collar existence. If you are making a big change in status, it is best to keep quiet for awhile anyway until you learn the ropes. Fortunately, it is a lot easier to fall into the vocabulary of your class than it is to change an accent or dialect.

It really isn't that practical to change one's features, which is often accomplished through plastic surgery. And if you make changes of your hair, facial hair, eyes (by wearing glasses or switching to contacts) you will also alter your features well enough to disguise yourself in most instances.

One exception would be scars or other glaring marks of identification. In many cases scars and other marks can be disguised with makeup or facial hair, and often as not the people who have them have been disguising them for years already. I met one disappearee who claimed to have had a spectacular set of buck teeth, so bad that, as he put it, he could "eat corn on the cob through a picket fence." The first thing he did when he vanished was have a dentist replace his protruding front teeth with a bridge, and it changed his appearance from night to day.

Hair dye for a man is often more trouble than it's worth. A dye job has to be continuously touched up or it becomes painfully obvious and a distraction to boot. The possible exception is for a man whose hair is bright orange because their aren't many people with naturally orange hair. A phone contact I made who was in this situation said he felt a cue-ball haircut was the best way to deal with it. He would rather run an electric razor over his head now and then than to always be monkeying around with a chemistry set. A hair dye job on a man will be talked about to no end if it is noticed, and talk is one thing the disappearee wants to avoid.

Location is a seldom appreciated method of personal identification, and it plays into the hands of the vanisher. One often fails to recognize them simply because they were expected to be elsewhere. And even if the disappearee is half-recognized the observer will be inclined to believe it is simply a case of mistaken identity if there is the least bit of disguise employed. And sometimes, even if there is no disguise at all.

SOME THINGS TO AVOID

The disappearee must be like a chameleon if he wants to stay a free man. That is, he must be able to blend in with his surroundings and avoid attracting attention to himself. If this fails and he finds himself being interrogated for some reason, a traffic violation, for example, he must be prepared with a reasonable-sounding life story that is backed up with some documentation. In short, the lamster must be prepared for identity checks at all times and proceed with caution to avoid them.

There are many cases of disappearees who have been able to outlast intensive investigations only to blow everything through an act of sheer stupidity.

Take the celebrated case of Patricia Hearst. Her kidnappers/companions were well known to the law enforcement folks, yet even the vaunted Federal Bureau of Investigation could not find hide nor hair of them for over a year. With all the money involved, and the fantastic amount of publicity surrounding the case, you can believe it was one of the most thorough manhunts ever launched. Yet a few of Miss Hearst's original group were only located and ventilated because one of them ripped off a pair of 98 cent socks in a sporting goods store!

For those who seriously desire to stay free, then, here are some tips from those who "have gone before."

The Paper Trail

Nobody, whether vanisher or "straight" can avoid laying a paper trail as he moves through life. The disappearee must be very careful in the initial stages of his new life not to make a slip. One mistake in documenting an identity could surface many years later, catching the disappearee off guard as he believes he has made it free and clear.

No matter what malarkey government agencies spout, all records, both private and official, must be presumed to be open to inspection by all comers. Social Security, withholding reports filed by employers, licenses, even Federal Income Tax returns are more or less open to the general public. And the information these records contain is *always* available to official investigative agencies.

Along these lines, withheld taxes are usually turned in by employers during April, July, October and January for the preceding quarter. This means that a man who works, even under his own name and Social Security number, in January, February and March can quit on April Fools Day and be on his way long before the reports that will pinpoint his location are processed.

Union pension plan payments and health and welfare contributions are often filed on a monthly basis and these records, too, are available for inspection. As a general rule, however, unions make a more conscientious effort to protect the privacy of their members than governmental agencies or commercial institutions.

An example of the extent to which snooping is conducted by so-called law enforcement agencies came to light recently when a well-to-do artist received a packet of cancelled checks from his bank. Neatly wrapped around the package was an interdepartmental memo addressed to the bank employees who process customers' monthly statements. It gave the artist's name and account number, then went on to say, "This memo is to authorize you to read checks to the FBI *before sending the statement to the customer.*" The italicized words were underlined in red ink.

The memo also contained the name and phone number of FBI agent Bud Watkins. While the FBI declined to comment on this item, Wells Fargo Bank admitted the memo was authentic. The artist was never charged with the commission of any crime. He believes the memo was included with his statement intentionally by a bank employee who wished him well.

The police blandly excuse their unlawful acts with the age-old alibi that they do it only for the greater public good. Of course, that's *their* interpretation of the public good. In their eyes this permits them to conduct illegal searches, seizures, bugging, beatings in back rooms, unlawful opening of first class mail, delving into supposedly confidential records and the like. And don't forget tapping telephones and accessing telephone company records.

The answer for the prudent disappearee should be self-evident. He must conduct himself with utmost propriety at all times and, as the late columnist Charles McCabe put it so well, "Stay out of government buildings insofar as possible."

Publicity

The disappearee should attempt to keep out of the public eye as much as possible. While we have already discussed the reasons for not taking a job as a TV reporter, radio announcer, bellhop or other highly public job, there are subtler ways that vanishers trip themselves up through publicity.

Stay away from public activities like rallies, marches, protests, etc. Such events are swarming with media photographers. You never know when you'll wake up one morning and see your smiling face on page one.

You should also avoid membership in publicity-seeking clubs. Their membership records may be available to the authorities or other investigators looking for you. A number of disappearees have been found when their pictures turned up in small club newsletters.

As a photographer myself, I can tell you that there are a great number of people who are absolute masters at avoiding the camera or spoiling shots. Their faces are always partially obscured by someone else's head or some object. And it happens enough that I know it is not coincidence; they watch out for cameras and keep themselves out of the line of fire.

Some people just run into bum luck and have their identities revealed. A good example of this is the old William Desmond Taylor murder case. Taylor was a top Hollywood movie director of his time who wound up murdered one day. In a case like this the police immediately make a thorough, painstaking investigation, starting from scratch. And scratch is, "Who was he?"

It turned out that Taylor was a disappearee who in his original identity had been a prosperous businessman from New York who had simply walked out of his life some years before. Since that time he served with distinction as an officer in the Canadian Army, had been in Alaska, and finally wound up as a movie director in Hollywood. His new identity was so well established that not much more was ever discovered. And his killer has not been identified to this day.

In the natural course of their investigation the police questioned his valet, a man who called himself "Sands." Sands was never a suspect himself. And as they had no particular reason to detain him, the police let him go, explaining that if they thought of more questions they would look him up.

They did think of some more questions, but they're probably still looking. For when Sands walked out of the police station he walked into oblivion and was never seen again. Many of the people involved in the case believe that Sands was Taylor's brother who had also disappeared some years before. An intensive search was mounted, but to no avail.

It was only through the incredible bad luck of Taylor's murder that any attention at all was ever paid to Sands.

Miscellaneous

A disappearee should never go about with more than one set of identification papers on his person. Any official questioning is likely to entail examination of the contents of the suspect's pockets. Nothing is going to be more immediately suspicious to an experienced officer than discovering that a suspect's ID is in two or three different names. Many petty criminals are tripped up on this point.

Obviously a disappearee should not carry contraband of any size, shape or description on his person, either inside the United States or outside. What is regarded as contraband varies greatly from country to country. In some parts of the world, being discovered with a Bible in your luggage would be grounds for detention.

By the same token, a disappearee should not attempt to pass various customs officers with a six-shooter on his person or in his luggage. This is especially important because handguns are flat *verboten* almost everywhere in the world including some states in the U.S. This most emphatically includes New York with the infamous Sullivan Act.

Detach With Your Past

It should go without saying that one of the prime requirements of a successful disappearance-cum-identity change is the complete divorcing of the new existence from the original. This is easier said than done, and some people just can't handle it at all.

Private detective agencies, police departments and skip-tracing firms have a myriad of ploys for locating vanishers, and almost without exception their tricks are based on the assumption that the missing person will eventually be foolish enough to communicate in some way, directly or indirectly, with one phase or another of his original existence. And in all too many instances they do just exactly that.

Take the sad example of the lamster who carried out a completely successful disappearance. Up to a point. In this case the man was an avid model boatbuilder, and he had no sooner established himself in his new life than he subscribed to the modelmaker's publications he'd read before he vanished. The private detective agency employed to find him assumed — correctly, as it turned out — that the subject might change everything else, but he wouldn't abandon his lifelong hobby. So the detectives

99

simply bought the mailing lists of the modelmaker's magazines and checked them for new subscribers. They could tell which were new and which were old by the coding on the mailing labels. As in any specialized field, subscribers tend to stay with their favorite publications year in and year out, and there aren't actually all that many new subscribers in any given month. The detectives checked the new subscribers against city and telephone directories, eliminating the ones who had been residents at the same address for any length of time. Of the very few who remained, one was their boy!

All moneys should be transferred from one identity to another in cash, using bills that are not too large. Even in today's overheated economy $100 bills are not all that common. Fifties, though, are rapidly on the increase, largely because some State Unemployment Compensation Offices pay their clients off with as many fifties as possible.

Travelers checks, cashier's checks, bank drafts and the like leave a trail between identities like a seven-dog team crossing a field of new-fallen snow. And they are sometimes hard for a man to cash before his new identity has had an opportunity to mature and "set."

And most emphatically, no gloating telephone calls to the abandoned spouse. It is better by far that he/she should feel sad or so-what than angry and/or resentful. The old saw about never stirring a hornet's nest with a stick goes triple here. Long distance phone calls are logged for billing purposes by the telephone companies as a matter of routine, although local calls aren't as a general rule. But even these leave a paper trail between the two telephones.

If for some reason it becomes necessary to mail something back to someone he knew in his original existence, then the vanisher should by all means use a remail service.

Remail services make a specialty of remailing letters and postcards for a fee, and almost invariably give prompt and satisfactory service. To locate a remail service, look in the classified ads of publications like Popular Mechanics, writers magazines, men's magazines, and any publication carrying low-cost classified ads. The charge for remailing is surprisingly nominal, and remailers are located pretty much all over the world. Some will even send their customers packets of local postcards to be filled out and returned to the remailer who then drops them in the mail at regular intervals, or as directed. See the *Directory of Mail Drops* in the reference chapter.

But remail service or no, the vanisher would be best advised not to do *any* communicating with his former life. Period.

Even to "keep track" of the activities of the abandoned family members can be a risk. I was astonished at the number of identity-changers who knew in minute detail what was going on in their previous existence!

And it should go without saying that no matter how tender the moment, or how great the temptation to confide, he should never divulge or even hint at the identity change to young ladies. Or not-so-young ladies. Exclamation Point! The old gag about the fastest methods of news dissemination being telephone and tell-a-woman is as true today as when it was coined some hundred years or so ago.

An astonishing number of disappearees violate this obvious and basic rule, to their ultimate sorrow, and identity-changers of all people, should know only too well how vindictive a woman can be when sufficiently provoked.

A little-appreciated facet of disappearing and identity switching is the extreme vulnerability of a vanisher to blackmail. And his absolute helplessness in the face of it, short of disappearing again.

A man died not too long ago down in Naples, Florida. He was the business manager for a family with extensive holdings throughout the country. Happily married, he and his wife were quite popular in the community.

Almost before his body cooled his "wife" spirited it out of town for burial. Whereupon the real Mrs. X turned up. Seemed our successful Floridan was really a disappearee out of Cleveland, Ohio.

In the resulting legal imbroglio a very interesting fact came to light. His original wife had been milking him for several hundred dollars a month for years as the price for keeping her mouth shut. How she managed to locate him in his new identity no one knows. My guess is that he was seen on the street by somebody who knew him in his original existence and promptly tipped off the original wife. Florida is, after all, an extremely poor choice for a vanisher from Cleveland because so many people from that city spend the cold weather months in Sunny Florida.

On his death the original wife made every effort to get her hands on his Florida estate, including the very home in which he had resided in bliss with his new lady. Fortunately for the latter he had anticipated this and had taken the proper legal steps to protect her rights. So the new "wife" was able to salvage at least some of the Florida holdings. Her popularity in the community helped in this, too.

The original wife, by the way, had managed to have him declared dead in Ohio and had collected his life insurance, in addition to the regular monthly payments she'd been bleeding him for. This in turn put her in a very interesting relationship with the insurance people!

POSTSCRIPT

On rereading the manuscript I've come to the conclusion that perhaps it is the men who *don't* disappear who should be pitied. They are the grouchy, embittered, ulcer-ridden men one sees every day, bound by ties of duty, loyalty and fear to a life they detest, hopeless in their forties, old before their time in their fifties.

In this age of loud and vocal minorities, the disappearees in our midst — and they are legion! — who constitute a minority group in every sense of the word, are refreshing in that they aren't hollering for handouts, howling about discrimination, or complaining about their lack of opportunity. And though in modern society the problems of an adult with no "paper background" are manifold and pressing, these people go calmly about overcoming their problems unaided, alone and with a complete absence of bitching.

And I believe it can be truly said that they are the only group that has come anywhere near to beating the system.

I salute them!

Doug Richmond

REFERENCES

The following books are good sources of further information on the topics discussed in this work.

MISSING PERSONS

SEARCH, by Jane Askin, Harper & Row, New York, 1982. *Written for adoptees searching for their biological parents, it discusses how paper trails many years old can be used to locate a person.*

HOW TO FIND MISSING PERSONS: A Handbook for Investigators, by Ronald George Eriksen 2, Loompanics Unlimited, Port Townsend, WA, 1984. *The definitive manual for skip tracers and private eyes.*

AMONG THE MISSING, by Jay Robert Nash, Simon and Schuster, New York, 1978. *Interesting stories on people who have disappeared permanently.*

ID IN AMERICA

THE PAPER TRIP I and THE PAPER TRIP II, Eden Press, Fountain Valley, CA, 1984 and 1985. *The classic and original books "For a New You through New ID."*

NEW I.D. IN AMERICA, by Anonymous, Paladin Press, Boulder, CO, 1983. *Excellent material, just what the title says.*

MAIL ORDER I.D., by Michael Hoy, Loompanics Unlimited, Port Townsend, WA, 1985. *Definitive guide to fake ID sold through the mail, with names & addresses of sellers, and photos of their products.*

ID IN OTHER COUNTRIES

HOW TO GET ID IN CANADA, by Ronald George Eriksen 2, Loompanics Unlimited, Port Townsend, WA, 1983. *This book is to Canada what the above books are to the USA.*

PAPER TRIPPING OVERSEAS: New I.D. in England, Australia and New Zealand, by Tony Newborn, Paladin Press, Boulder, CO, 1985. *The title is self-explanatory.*

FINDING WORK

HOW TO STEAL A JOB, by Bill Conners, Financial Management Associates, Phoenix, AZ, 1977. *A good book on the "hidden" job market, with a good section on how to create a fake job history.*

TEMPORARY EMPLOYMENT: The Flexible Alternative, by Demaris C. Smith, Betterway Publications, White Hall, VA, 1985. *Excellent guide to finding temporary employment.*

GUERRILLA CAPITALISM: How to Practice Free Enterprise in an Unfree Economy, by Adam Cash, Loompanics Unlimited, Port Townsend, WA, 1984. *The definitive guide to evading taxes and keeping a low profile in the Underground Economy.*

HOW TO DO BUSINESS "OFF THE BOOKS", by Adam Cash, Loompanics Unlimited, Port Townsend, WA, 1986. *Just what the title says — the sequel to the above book.*

GETTING CREDIT

THE COMPLETE CREDIT BOOK, by Bruce Brown & Tom Nelson, Inflation Reports, Los Angeles, 1986. *A fine guide to obtaining credit, including how to get a Visa or Mastercard with no credit check.*

CREDIT, Eden Press, Fountain Valley Ca, 1984. *Excellent book on how to get credit in America.*

PRIVACY AND STAYING FREE

PERSONAL AND BUSINESS PRIVACY, by Bill Pryor, Eden Press, Fountain Valley, CA, 1986. *How to keep the snoopers away from you.*

PRIVACY: How to Get it; How to Enjoy it, by Bill Kaysing, Eden Press, Fountain Valley, CA, 1977. *Excellent book on personal privacy.*

DIRECTORY OF MAIL DROPS IN THE UNITED STATES AND CANADA (With an Appendix for Foreign Countries), compiled by Michael Hoy, Loompanics Unlimited, Port Townsend, WA, current edition. *A listing of over 700 mail drops and remailing services all over the world, descriptions of their services, and tips on using them.*

METHODS OF DISGUISE, by John Sample, Loompanics Unlimited, Port Townsend, WA, 1984. *Everything there is to know about disguising oneself.*

LOW PROFILE, by William Petrocelli, McGraw-Hill, 1981. *How to avoid the privacy invaders.*

HOW I FOUND FREEDOM IN AN UNFREE WORLD, by Harry Browne, Avon Books, New York, 1973. *The best guide to thinking like a free person — how to live your life the way you want to live it.*

HOW TO HIDE ANYTHING, by Michael Conner, Paladin Press, Boulder, CO, 1984. *Just what the title says.*

YOU WILL ALSO WANT TO READ:

CONTROVERSIAL AND UNUSUAL BOOKS!!!

"Yes, there are books about the skills of apocalypse -- spying, surveillance, fraud, wire-tapping, smuggling, self-defense, lockpicking, gunmanship, eavesdropping, car chasing, civil warfare, surviving jail, and dropping out of sight. Apparently writing books is the way mercenaries bring in spare cash between wars. The books are useful, and it's good the information is freely available (and they definitely inspire interesting dreams), but their advice should be taken with a salt shaker or two and all your wits. A few of these volumes are truly scary. Loompanics is the best of the Libertarian suppliers who carry them. Though full of 'you'll-wish-you'd-read-these-when-it's-too-late' rhetoric, their catalog is genuinely informative."
-THE NEXT WHOLE EARTH CATALOG

Now available:
THE BEST BOOK CATALOG IN THE WORLD!!!

- *Large 8½ x 11 size!*
- *More than 500 of the most controversial and unusual books ever printed!!!*
- *YOU can order EVERY book listed!!!*
- *Periodic Supplements to keep you posted on the LATEST titles available!!!*

We offer hard-to-find books on the world's most unusual subjects. Here are a few of the topics covered IN DEPTH in our exciting new catalog:

- *Hiding/concealment of physical objects! A complete section of the best books ever written on hiding things!*
- *Fake ID/Alternate Identities! The most comprehensive selection of books on this little-known subject ever offered for sale! You have to see it to believe it!*
- *Investigative/Undercover methods and techniques! Professional secrets known only to a few, now revealed for YOU to use! Actual police manuals on shadowing and surveillance!*
- *And much, much more, including Locks and Locksmithing, Self Defense, Intelligence Increase, Life Extension, Money-Making Opportunities, and much, much more!*

Our book catalog is truly THE BEST BOOK CATALOG IN THE WORLD! Order yours today -- you will be very pleased, we know.

(Our catalog is free with the order of any book on the previous page -- or is $2.00 if ordered by itself.)

**Loompanics Unlimited
PO Box 1197
Pt Townsend, WA 98368
USA**